THE AMERICAN
LABOR MOVEMENT

INTERPRETATIONS OF AMERICAN HISTORY

★ ★ ★ JOHN HIGHAM AND BRADFORD PERKINS, EDITORS

THE AMERICAN
LABOR MOVEMENT

EDITED BY

DAVID BRODY

University of California, Davis

HARPER & ROW, PUBLISHERS
NEW YORK   EVANSTON   SAN FRANCISCO   LONDON

CONTENTS

v

EDITORS' INTRODUCTION

This volume—and companions in the series, "Interpretations of American History"—makes a special effort to cope with one of the basic dilemmas confronting every student of history. On the one hand, historical knowledge shares a characteristic common to all appraisals of human affairs. It is partial and selective. It picks out some features and facts of a situation while ignoring others that may be equally pertinent. The more selective an interpretation is, the more memorable and widely applicable it can be. On the other hand, history has to provide what nothing else does: a total estimate, a multifaceted synthesis, of man's experience in particular times and places. To study history, therefore, is to strive simultaneously for a clear, selective focus and for an integrated, over-all view.

In that spirit, each volume of the series aims to resolve the varied literature on a major topic or event into a meaningful whole. One interpretation, we believe, does not deserve as much of a student's attention as another simply because they are in conflict. Instead of contriving a balance between opposing views, or choosing polemical material simply to create an appearance of controversy, David Brody has exercised his own judgment on the relative importance of different aspects or interpretations of a problem. We have asked him to select some of what he considers the best, most persuasive writings bearing on the American labor movement, indicating in the introductory essay and headnotes his reasons for considering these accounts convincing or significant. When appropriate, he has also brought out the relation between older and more recent approaches to the subject. The editor's own competence and experience in the field enable him to provide a sense of order and to indicate the evolution and complexity of interpretations. He is, then, like other editors in this series, an informed participant rather than a mere observer, a student sharing with other students the results of his own investigations of the literature on a crucial phase of American development.

JOHN HIGHAM
BRADFORD PERKINS

THE AMERICAN
LABOR MOVEMENT

INTRODUCTION

"We have no ultimate ends. We are going on from day to day. We are fighting only for immediate objects—objects that can be realized in a few years. . . . We want to dress better and to live better, and become better off. . . . We are opposed to theorists. . . . We are all practical men." So spoke the pioneer trade unionist Adolph Strasser before a Congressional committee in 1885. His words defined the essence of the American trade unionism that was just then coming into its own. Here was a labor movement that restricted its horizon to advancing the day-to-day job interests of its members; that explicitly denied any interest in changing the existing economic order; that stressed realism in shaping its institutions and in dealing with employers; that insisted on the need for labor power, limited however to economic weapons and utilized only in the context of collective bargaining; that ruled political action out as a primary method and, concomitantly, considered labor's problems no proper concern of government; and that boasted of having no room for intellectuals or patience with social theories. None of these elements was quite as clear-cut in practice as they sounded in the oratory of Samuel Gompers. Nor were any of them wholly absent from the European movements. But the characteristics, dominant as they were and combined as they were, added up to a uniquely American form of trade unionism.

This fact invested the labor movement with a special fascination from the very first. What accounted for the uniqueness? The question was asked, in one form or another, by every serious student of American labor

—not to speak of the postmortems by frustrated generations of the American left who had failed to win over the trade unions to politics and revolution.

Labor history as a scholarly subject had its start under the aegis of John R. Commons of the University of Wisconsin. Under his direction, the scattered records of American labor and trade unionism were gathered and published in the monumental eleven-volume *A Documentary History of American Industrial Society* (1910–1911). From that base, it became possible for the first time to write labor's history. *The History of Labour in the United States* (1918–1935), which Commons planned and guided, remains today the standard account for the period it covers, that is, up to 1932. Commons' primary historiographical contribution was to establish the framework in which historical analysis could take place. One of the founders of institutional economics, Commons helped rescue the study of labor from the deadly embrace of classical economics. An important practical thrust impelled Commons' efforts: he was warding off the conservative charge that trade unionism violated the sacred mechanisms of the market place. The realities of labor-management relations, Commons argued, bore little resemblance to the abstractions of classical economics. (Who could really believe that individual workingmen and corporate employers bargained on equal terms?) Trade unionism, he insisted, performed the necessary jobs of equalizing the bargaining relationship and of bringing "a common law of labor" into the factory. It was especially to reveal the roots and causes of labor's real world that Commons turned his attention to history (as did so many other economists who rebelled against the *a priori* doctrines of classical economics).

Of Commons' specific contributions, the most lasting traced the origins of American trade unionism. Like Sidney and Beatrice Webb, Commons focused on the differentiation of classes. He tied the emergence of the American working class to the expansion of the market: as the transportation revolution broke open local market monopolies, the functions of merchant, manufacturer and worker—hitherto combined in the single craftsman—separated, and the competition that accompanied widening markets in turn forced wages and working conditions down—hence the appearance of trade unionism. Commons' demonstration of this process in his classic essay, "American Shoemakers, 1648–1895," remains as persuasive today as when it was written over half a century ago. Commons also had a good deal to say about the behavior of American unions: on universal suffrage as an inhibiter of labor politics; on the federal system of government as a cause for the union assumption of responsibility for uniform standards; on immigration and mechanization as reasons for the American emphasis on the closed shop. But John R. Commons never developed a general interpretation to explain the character of the American labor movement.

This task he left to his student and successor at Wisconsin, Selig Perlman. *A Theory of the Labor Movement* (1928) represents the most comprehensive attempt in our literature to interpret American trade unionism. (It is, in fact, even more ambitious, since it aims at a thesis applicable to all labor movements; however, only its treatment of American unions has had lasting influence.) Perlman placed the role of the intellectual at the center of his *Theory*. There was, Perlman insisted, a "basic contradiction . . . between the mentality of organic labor and that of the revolutionary intellectual." The chief characteristic of the latter was to regard "labor as an 'abstract' mass in the grip of an abstract 'force'." The intellectuals considered it their appointed task to show labor the way. (Lenin's dictum exemplified the intellectual viewpoint in Perlman's eyes: "Left to its own forces, the working class can only attain trade-union consciousness." And likewise the Socialist theoretician Karl Kautsky: "Socialist consciousness is something introduced from without, and not something that arose spontaneously.") Labor movements dominated by such men might go in any one of several politico-revolutionary directions—all mapped out in detail by Perlman. The crucial point, however, was that the choice did not spring from the working class itself. And what if a labor movement escaped the clutches of the intellectuals? Then it would develop "organically" from the needs and desires of the rank-and-file. This, said Perlman, was the fortunate American experience. The viewpoint of the workingman was "job-conscious," and his overriding desire was to regulate access to employment. "The trade unionism of the American Federation of Labor was a shift from an optimistic psychology, reflecting the abundance of opportunity in a partly settled continent, to the more pessimistic trade-union psychology, built upon the premise that the wage-earner is faced by a scarcity of opportunity." From these basic circumstances—a job-conscious constituency in an age of apparently shrinking job opportunity and the development of labor institutions and policies responsive to that wage-earning constituency free from the influence of middle-class intellectuals —all else followed in the shaping of American pure-and-simple unionism.

The Wisconsin theory was hardly the last word on the subject. Perlman wrote from the perspective of the 1920s. The year after he published the *Theory,* the Great Depression began. American capitalism foundered to a degree wholly unanticipated in the New Era. The labor movement broke out of its craft-union mold, and swiftly encompassed the mass-production workers after 1935. Government intervened decisively in the area of labor relations. And then World War II initiated a period of labor prosperity that called into question the old assumptions of job scarcity. In the early

1950s, Perlman's thesis came under intensive scholarly scrutiny.[1] To what extent did the *Theory* still apply? Two related questions were really being asked. Was Perlman's characterization of the labor movement still accurate? The emphasis here was on the emergence of the Congress of Industrial Organizations. Given its evident commitment to broader social objectives, its willingness to engage in partisan politics, and its encouragement of government involvement in the labor sphere, could the CIO be characterized as pure-and-simple trade unionism? The second question touched the circumstances within which organized labor operated. Had not the changes since the 1920s—the incorporation of millions of mass-production workers, the development of an economy in which job scarcity no longer seemed inevitable, and the immense expansion of the public role both in setting the terms of labor-management relations and by social legislation that secured labor's well-being directly—been so far-reaching as to render Perlman's analysis inapplicable?

No consensus emerged at the time between critics and defenders. Perlman himself insisted that the external changes, massive although they were, had not altered the primary direction of the labor movement. At an Industrial Relations Research Association symposium on the *Theory*, Perlman said: "In the grasp of the Wisconsin School, the American labor program, indicative of its basic philosophy, has shown remarkable steadfastness through times of rapid external change. The objective . . . is unaltered from Gompers' day; the methods, even outside the immediate vicinity of the job, show no more change than could be accounted for by the changing environment." Since those words were spoken in 1950, the course of events would seem on the whole to have sustained Perlman's contention. The fate of the CIO, even before it merged with the American Federation of Labor in 1955, revealed the powerful grip that the pure-and-simple philosophy still exerted on American organized labor. On the other hand, labor's political role, its community involvements, its modern patterns of organizing and collective bargaining reveal changes of sufficient degree, if not of kind, as to demand a major reassessment: precisely

[1] See the following: "Theory of the Labor Movement: A Reappraisal," Industrial Relations Research Association, *Proceedings of the Third Annual Meeting* (December 28–29, 1950), pp. 140–183; Philip Taft, "A Rereading of Selig Perlman's 'A Theory of the Labor Movement,'" *Industrial and Labor Relations Review*, IV (October, 1950), pp. 70–77; Industrial Relations Research Association, *Interpreting the Labor Movement* (Madison, Wisconsin, 1952); Charles A. Gulick and Melvin K. Bers, "Insight and Illusion in Perlman's Theory of the Labor Movement," *Industrial and Labor Relations Review*, VI (July, 1953), pp. 510–531; Adolf Sturmthal, "Comments on Selig Perlman's 'A Theory of the Labor Movement,'" *Industrial and Labor Relations Review*, IV (July, 1951), pp. 483–496.

what are the continuities between the labor movement of 1928 and that of 1970?

The Wisconsin theory poses another question. Granting the essential correctness of its characterization of the labor movement, how persuasive does the underlying explanation remain? Perlman's analysis derived from a particular scholarly perspective. Institutional economics took as its special mission the replacement of abstract, *a priori* analysis by empirical investigation that emphasized the organic development of economic institutions. Perlman's stress on the role of the intellectuals represented, in fact, an interesting evolution of his teacher's views on classical economics. Commons attacked the abstract, theoretical study of labor. Perlman took this bias and placed it within the stream of history itself. His hostility to doctrinaire labor intellectuals—the "expert astrologers"—was really a counterpart to Commons' distaste for doctrinaire economics. Can modern scholars accept the absence of the intellectuals' domination as decisive in the development of the labor movement? Why, for that matter, was it so resistant to the radical intellectuals? Similarly on the matter of job-consciousness. Was the sense of job scarcity so pervasive as Perlman believed? What of the unionized non-craft occupations to which access could not be controlled by trade unions? What of the times (such as the period of World War I) when there was genuine labor scarcity? Writing in the context of the 1920s, Perlman probably accepted too readily the prevailing circumstances as permanent and immutable. Clearly, the Wisconsin theory, for all its wisdom and insight, is a dated statement that needs to be redone in the modern perspective.

No one has yet undertaken—or, at least, completed—that large task. Perhaps it is just as well. Ideally, a comprehensive interpretation of the labor movement should arise out of the best that modern scholarship has to offer. The groundwork, however, is still being laid on which to build a new interpretation. This collection is really in the nature of an interim report. It is an attempt to bring together some of the results of recent scholarship that, in one way or another, throw new light on the character and development of the labor movement. The approaches cover a wide range. Two authors—S. M. Lipset and Melvin Dubofsky—inquire directly into the socioeconomic sources of American labor organization. One—Michael Rogin—closely reexamines the trade-union doctrine of voluntarism. Two—David Brody and Ray Marshall—try to explain labor strategy relating to unionization and race relations. The other three—Gerald Grob, Robert Christie and John Laslett—do detailed historical analyses of key points of trade-union development. What all these essays have in common, varying as they do in focus, is a sensitivity to the basic interpretive issues of American trade unionism. All of them have something fresh to say about the shaping of the labor movement. They reveal, too, the range of modern scholarship that is being brought to bear on the subject. Here are an eminent sociologist (Lipset), a brilliant young political scientist (Rogin), a labor economist (Marshall) and five professional historians applying the tools of their trades to the study of trade-union development. It is a far cry from the institutional economics that has hitherto dominated the study of this segment of American history.

The essays in this collection, as I have said, do not replace the Wisconsin theory. But they are the stuff from which a new interpretation will come. Who knows? Perhaps a student reading these essays will see in them some crucial link that will provide the basis for the new theory of the American labor movement.

Trade Unionism and the American Social Order

SEYMOUR MARTIN LIPSET

In this essay, the sociologist S. M. Lipset addresses himself to the most central question in the study of American trade unionism. How has the social order shaped the labor movement? In one form or another, every serious student in the field has asked this question. What makes Lipset's essay distinctive is his rigorous approach to the issue and his attempt to establish the connections at the most basic social level. Earlier in his book *The First New Nation,* Lipset isolated two determining American values—equality and achievement. In this chapter on trade unionism (as in a preceding one on American religion), he demonstrates the institutional consequences. In the case of the labor movement, Lipset suggests that the equalitarian-achievement orientation excluded a class-conscious ideology, emphasized immediate, material goals, and encouraged militant tactics. Most striking, perhaps, was the generating of a cadre of career leaders. Using comparative data from six labor movements, Lipset discovers that American trade unions employ by far the largest number of full-time officers in relation to membership. Although marking only a start, Lipset's pioneering essay suggests the possibilities inherent in a rigorous analysis of the relationship between the social order and the American labor movement.

ALTHOUGH MANY MAY ARGUE WITH MY STRESS ON THE CONTINUITY of the essential traits of American character and religion, few would question the thesis that our business institutions have reflected the constant emphasis in the American value system on individual achievement. From the earliest comments of foreign travelers down to the present,

From Seymour Martin Lipset, *The First New Nation,* New York: Basic Books, Inc., 1963, pp. 170–199. © by S. M. Lipset. Reprinted by permission of the publisher. Footnotes have been omitted except where they amplify the text.

men have identified a strong materialistic bent as being a characteristic American trait. The worship of the dollar, the desire to make a profit, the effort to get ahead through the accumulation of wealth, all have been credited to the egalitarian character of the society, that is, to the absence of aristocracy. As Tocqueville noted in his discussion of the consequences of a democracy's destruction of aristocracy: "They have swept away the privileges of some of their fellow creatures which stood in their way, but they have opened the door to universal competition." And the study of the comments on American workers of various nineteenth-century foreign travelers cited earlier notes that most of these European writers, among whom were a number of socialists, concluded that "social and economic democracy in America, far from mitigating competition for social status, intensified it. . . ."

American secular and religious values both have facilitated the "triumph of American capitalism," and have fostered status striving. The focus on equalitarianism and individual opportunity has also prevented the emergence of class consciousness among the lower classes. The absence of a socialist or labor party, and the historic weakness of American trade-unionism, appear to attest to the strength of values which depreciated a concern with class. The growth of a large trade-union movement during the 1930's, together with the greater political involvement of labor organizations in the Democratic party, suggested to some that the day—long predicted by many Marxists—was arriving in which the American working class would finally follow in the footsteps of its European brethren. Such changes in the structure of class relations seemed to these observers to reflect the decline of opportunity and the hardening of class lines. To them such changes could not occur without modification in the traditional value system, that is, without a decline in the stress on equality and achievement.

A close examination of the character of the American labor movement, however, suggests that it, like the church, may be perceived as reflecting the basic values of the larger society. Although unions, like all other American institutions, have changed in various ways congruent with the growth of an urban industrial civilization, the essential traits of American trade unions, as of business corporations, may still be derived from key elements in the American value system.

Since a large labor movement is of relatively recent vintage in American society, I shall not try to trace historical continuities in its behavior and structure. Rather, I shall attempt to specify how the character of American unions differs from those in other industrial countries, and to account for these differences by analyzing the relationship between labor movements and the social structures of these nations. In moving from a more historical to a more comparative approach, I have purposely limited the scope of the comparison to those countries which most resemble the United States in economic and political organization.

The union movements compared are all located in industrially developed nations which have relatively stable democratic political systems. They are characterized by "the uninterrupted continuation of political democracy since World War I *and* the absence of a major political movement opposed to the democratic 'rules of the game.'" They are also similar in the assumptions they make about the role of unions and the nature of industrial relations. The labor movements of these countries all assume, more or less, as Hugh Clegg has recently put it, that "unions must be independent both of the state and of management . . . , that only the unions can represent the industrial interests of workers . . . [and] that the ownership of industry is irrelevant to good industrial relations." These nations are "the United States, Britain, Scandinavia, Holland, Switzerland, Australia, Canada, and New Zealand."

Although the American labor movement is similar to others in many respects, it differs from those of the other stable democracies in ideology, class solidarity, tactics, organizational structure, and patterns of leadership behavior. American unions are more conservative; they are more narrowly self-interested; their tactics are more militant; they are more decentralized in their collective bargaining; and they have many more full-time salaried officials, who are on the whole much more highly paid and who exhibit a somewhat greater penchant to engage in corrupt practices. American unions have also organized a smaller proportion of the labor force than have unions in these other nations.

In stressing variations between American unionism and that of other countries, particularly those of northwestern Europe and Australasia, I do not mean to imply that any of these differences are of such magnitude as to make American unionism a qualitatively different phenomenon from the others. Clearly, the labor movements in all industrialized democracies have great similarities and perform similar functions. Although American unions are less class conscious politically than those of Europe, they are certainly involved in politics.[1] American labor leaders earn more relative

---

[1] Their relations with the Democratic Party resemble those of many European unions with their socialist parties. However, as George Cyriax and Robert Oakeshott note: "The fact still remains that the British unions are 'in politics' in a sense in which their United States counterparts are definitely not. Their leaders still subscribe to a large body of Socialist objectives which can only be achieved through political action. . . . In America, by contrast, there is no distinct set of political beliefs superimposed on the informal working arrangements between the unions and the Democratic Party. Formally, therefore, the AFL-CIO is not affiliated to any party, and only tends to become involved in active politics when anti-union legislation is in the air."

to the rank and file than do European labor leaders, but the perquisites of the latter are also quite considerable in the form of high status, power, interesting work, travel, and the like. With the possible exception of leadership corruption and involvement in private business, almost every practice which may be mentioned as characteristic of American unionism is to be found in the northwestern European or Australasian movements. Clearly, as Clegg indicates, the labor movements of this industrialized, democratic "culture area" resemble each other greatly when contrasted with the types of movements found in southern and Latin Europe and in the underdeveloped states. But it is obvious also that considerable differences do exist between the labor movement of the United States and those of other countries in its "culture area."

SOCIAL STRUCTURE: THE SOURCE OF AMERICAN UNIONISM

In order to explain, in part, why American unionism differs from the unionism of the other predominantly Protestant, industrial democracies of northwestern Europe and Australasia, it is necessary to describe in more detail the way in which the trade union, as an American institution, has responded to and reflected the pressures generated by the interplay between America's basic values and the facts of social stratification in an industrial society. The stress on equality and achievement in American society has meant that Americans are much more likely to be concerned with the achievement of approved *ends*—particularly pecuniary success— than with the use of appropriate *means*—the behavior considered appropriate to a given position or status. In a country which stresses success above all, men are led to feel that the most important thing is to win the game, regardless of the methods employed in doing so. American culture applies the norms of a completely competitive society to everyone. Winners take all. As Robert K. Merton has put it:

> What makes American culture relatively distinctive . . . is that it is "a society which places a high premium on economic affluence and social ascent for all its members." . . . This patterned expectation is regarded as appropriate for everyone, irrespective of his initial lot or station in life. . . .
> This leads naturally to the subsidiary theme that success or failure are results wholly of personal qualities, that he who fails has only himself to blame, for the corollary to the concept of the self-made man is the self-unmade man. To the extent that his cultural definition is assimilated by those who have not made their mark, failure represents a double defeat: the manifest defeat of remaining far behind in the race for success and

the implicit defeat of not having the capacities and moral stamina needed for success. . . . It is in this cultural setting that, in a significant proportion of cases, the threat of defeat motivates men to the use of those tactics, beyond the law or the mores, which promise "success."

The moral mandate to achieve success thus exerts pressure to succeed, by fair means if possible and by foul means if necessary.

In contrast, one of the essential norms in more traditionalistic, ascriptive, or aristocratic societies is that one should behave in a manner appropriate to one's station. In the morality of aristocracy, to play the game well is more important than victory. All privileged strata seek to develop norms which justify their right to high status and which limit, if they do not eliminate, the possibility that they may be supplanted by "new men," by the upwardly mobile who succeed by "innovating"—that is, by ignoring the conventions. To emphasize correct behavior, manners, and so forth, is to reward the characteristics which those born to privilege are most likely to have. And since it is part of the logic of family life and social stratification to desire to perpetuate if not enhance the status of children and other family members, there is constant pressure in all societies to create "aristocratic" norms, or to preserve them if they have been handed down from previous eras, as has been the case for most European countries.

Because of its revolutionary origins, America entered the era of a capitalist, industrial, and politically democratic society without the traditions of an aristocratic or deferential order. As a result, the norms of aristocracy, though present to a limited extent among the social elite, have not been able to make much headway. The tendency of the successful achievers to undermine equality has been checked by the recurrent victories of the forces of equality in the political order. Capitalism and industrialism have reinforced equalitarian forces in this struggle: a market economy operates best under conditions of free competition, recognizing neither family background nor social limitations.

In a society with aristocratic origins, where norms derived from a pre-industrial social system still retain force and where they have often been partly accepted by the newer upper class of industrial society, there is greater emphasis on the propriety of class consciousness. Such a society, which places less emphasis on general achievement by everyone regardless of background, usually incorporates more *particular* sets of goals for each major social stratum. Thus a worker who is the son of a worker is less likely to view himself a personal failure than is a comparably situated man in a more equalitarian and achievement-oriented culture such as that of the United States. The weaker sense of personal failure felt by lower stratum individuals in such a "particularistic" social order does not mean that they feel less resentment over having inferior status, but rather that they are less likely to feel personally responsible for their "failure" or to feel the need to do something extraordinary about it. Deprived individuals are more likely to try to improve their situations *collectively* through social movements and class-conscious political parties. Or to put it in descriptive terms: in an achievement-oriented society such as the United States, the lower status person is more likely to feel impelled to drive *himself* to get ahead; in the more ascriptive European cultures, there will be greater emphasis on collective modification of the class structure.[2]

Since the emphasis is on individual success in the United States, those individuals or groups who feel themselves handicapped and who seek to resolve their consequent doubts about their personal worth are under strong pressure to "innovate," that is, to use whatever means they can find to gain recognition. This pressure to innovate may be reflected in efforts which established groups would not make—for example, the development of new and risky industries by those of recent immigrant background and low status who are barred, by limited economic resources and social discrimination, from advancing up economic ladders.[3] Similarly, urban machine politics, which required the use of "unconventional" tactics, became a road to success for various immigrant groups.

The pressure to succeed may also lead individuals and groups to serve social needs which are *outside* the law, in occupations usually described as "rackets." Organized vice—prostitution, bootlegging, and gambling—has been open to ambitious individuals from deprived social backgrounds when other fields were closed. The rackets have attracted members of minority ethnic groups who are strongly motivated by the American emphasis on achievement, but who are limited in their access to legitimate means of succeeding. Members of groups engaged in illegitimate businesses often do not conceive of themselves as engaged in crime, but rather as conforming to the achievement norms.

Criminal activities and corrupt politics may be found to some extent in all countries and may be more prevalent in impoverished regions of the world, such as Asia, southern Europe, and Latin America; but within the general culture area of the predominantly Protestant, relatively affluent, industrialized nations of northwestern Europe and the English-speaking countries of the Commonwealth, the United States is well out in the lead.

---

[2] Of course, these are only relative comparisons; Euorpeans try to get ahead, and Americans try to change the distribution of privilege. It is the difference in emphasis that I stress here.

[3] The Jews, for example, played a major role in developing the motion picture industry and in introducing credit practices in retailing selling.

As many observers have pointed out, the comparatively high crime rate in America, both in the form of lower-class rackets and white-collar and business defalcation, may be perceived as a consequence of the stress laid on success. Daniel Bell, for example, has suggested that racketeering may be seen as a natural by-product of American culture:

> Crime, in many ways, is a Coney Island mirror, caricaturing the morals and manners of a society. The jungle quality of the American business community, particularly at the turn of the century, was reflected in the mode of "business" practiced by the coarse gangster elements, most of them from new immigrant families, who were "getting ahead," just as Horatio Alger had urged. . . .
>
> The desires satisfied in extra-legal fashion were more than a hunger for the "forbidden fruits" of conventional morality. They also involved in the complex and ever shifting structure of group, class, and ethnic stratification, which is the warp and woof of America's "open" society, such "normal" goals as independence through a business of one's own, and such "moral" aspirations as the desire for social advancement and social prestige. For crime, in the language of the sociologists, has a "functional" role in the society, and the urban rackets—the illicit activity organized for continuing profit, rather than individual illegal acts— . . . [are] one of the queer ladders of social mobility in American life.

Given the extent of the pressure to "innovate," it is not surprising to find evidence that the successful may win general acceptance even if there is public knowledge that they used extralegal methods to get ahead. In the mid-nineteenth century, Charles Dickens commented that in America:

> The merits of a broken speculation, or a bankruptcy, or of a successful scoundrel, are not gauged by its or his observance of the golden rule, "Do as you would be done by," but are considered with reference to their smartness. . . . The following dialogue I have held a hundred times: "Is it not a very disgraceful circumstance that such a man as So-and-So should be acquiring a large property by the most infamous and odious maens, and notwithstanding all the crimes of which he has been guilty, should be tolerated and abetted by your citizens? He is a public nuisance, is he not?" "Yes, Sir." "A convicted liar?" "Yes, Sir." "He has been kicked, and cuffed, and caned?" "Yes, Sir." "And he is utterly dishonourable, debased, and profligate?" "Yes, Sir." "In the name of wonder, then, what is his merit?" "Well, Sir, he is a smart man."

A study of a Boston election in the 1940's in which James Curley was re-elected mayor while under a charge of fraud (for which he was subsequently convicted) reported that there was a general image among his supporters, who were aware of the charges of dishonesty, that he "gets things done."

SOCIETAL VALUES AND THE UNION MOVEMENT

The Relative Lack of Class Consciousness and the
Self-Interest of Individual Unions

The lack of a class-conscious ideology in the American labor movement may be directly traced to the equalitarian, anti-class orientation of the values associated with America's national identity. Thus it may be suggested that one of the reasons unions have had trouble organizing new segments of the employed population as compared to unions in northern Europe is that they have been handicapped by their slightly illegitimate position relative to the value system. "Union" connotes "class" organization.

In an interesting effort to account for the failure of socialism to take root in American society, Leon Samson has suggested that an important cause has been that Americanism is a political ideology with much the same value content as socialism. It endorses the progress of the society toward the more equal distribution of privileges that socialism demands. As a result, the rank and file members of American labor unions have not had to look for an ideology that justified the changes which they desired in the society.

However, the failure of the American labor movement to identify itself as a class movement may be traced more directly to the way in which equalitarianism and achievement orientation permeated the social structure. As Schumpeter has noted, the self-interested orientation of the American labor movement is but the application, in the realm of working-class life and trade unions, of the general value scheme. *Indeed, instead of reducing the individualistic orientation that Marxism associates with the early phase of capitalism, increasing industrialization in American society has reinforced the egalitarian-achievement attitudes toward stratification that early became part of the American national character.* In a sense, industrialization has lent these attitudes continued legitimacy: industrialization and advancing technology brought about an almost unbroken increase in national wealth on both an absolute and a per capita basis, so that in the nineteenth century America became the wealthiest country in the world, a position it has never relinquished.[4] And as David

---

[4] Between 1869 and 1953 per capita annual income (standardized to 1929 prices) rose from $215 to $1,043. The gross national product increased five times from 1890 to 1950 as a result of a two-fold increase in population and a three-fold rise in labor productivity. This increase in the gross national product has, in turn, meant that the average income per consumption unit increased. In 1929, it was $4,190 per year, standardized to 1960 prices; in 1954, it was $6,730.

Potter has well stressed, the fact of increasing abundance, no matter how unequally distributed, has served to permit the majority of the American population, including most trade-unionists, to enjoy a visible living standard roughly comparable among all groups with the exception of the extremely wealthy:

> American social distinctions, however real they may be and however difficult to break down, are not based upon or supported by great disparities in wealth, in education, in speech, in dress, etc., as they are in the old world. If the American class structure is in reality very unlike the classless society which we imagine, it is equally unlike the formalized class societies of former times. . . . The factor of abundance has . . . constantly operated to equalize the overt differences between the various classes. . . .

Within this context the very success of trade unions in improving the relative position of their members *vis à vis* other groups in the population has simply contributed to the maintenance of their members' belief in the American value system.

The Militant Tactics of Unions

Just as ideological conservatism and pursuit of narrow self-interests may be derived from the value system, so may the use of violent and militant tactics. Here the labor movement, like American business, reflects the social system's relatively greater emphasis on ends as contrasted with means. One tries to win economic and social objectives by whatever means are at hand. The fact that American workers are sufficiently dissatisfied with their economic conditions to tolerate relatively frequent, long, and bitter strikes may also be explained by reference to the social structure and its values. In summing up the conclusions of late nineteenth-century foreign visitors to America, Robert Smuts points out that they saw it in this light:

> The frequency and the bitterness of industrial conflict was the most basic fault the foreigners found in American industrial life. . . .
> Most of the European visitors explained industrial conflict as a result rather than a contradiction of the material and social democracy which typified the life of the American worker. The abundance of his life, they pointed out, added to the strength of his ambition for more. His self-reliance made him sensitive to his rights. Industrial conflict in America was a man-to-man fight, with no quarter asked or given, unmitigated by the tradition of subordination on the one hand, or of benevolence and responsibility on the other.

It may also be argued that we should expect more *individual* discontent with income and position among workers in America than within the more rigidly and visibly stratified European countries. The more rigid the stratification of a nation, the more candid the emphasis on the existence of differences among classes, the greater the extent to which lower status individuals will be likely to contrast their lot—*as a class*—with that of the more privileged classes. On the other hand, in a more loosely structured class system, people will be more prone to compare themselves *individually* with other workers who are relatively close to them in income and status. Thus if, in the latter system, groups or individuals improve their status, there will be resentment on the part of those left behind.

In other words, an open-class system leads workers to resent inequalities in income and status between themselves and others more frequently than does an ascriptively stratified system, where the only inequalities that count are class inequalities. America's equalitarian value system, by less clearly defining the range of groups with which workers may legitimately compare themselves, can make for greater individual discontent among workers than is the case in Europe. European social structure, by regarding labor, in the words of Winston Churchill, as "an estate of the realm," makes clear to workers why they are lowly and calls upon them to act collectively; American social structure, by eschewing estates, creating vague and even illegitimate class boundaries, and stressing equality, blames individuals for being lowly and calls upon them to alleviate their resentment by improving their status in as self-interested and narrowly defined terms as possible. John L. Lewis, founder of the Congress of Industrial Organizations, president of the United Mine Workers for nearly forty years, and perhaps the most militant labor leader in the United States since the 1920's was a Republican most of his life and a strong advocate of conservative, *laissez-faire* economics (although he was willing to use state power to bolster his union and the coal industry).

There is some evidence in support of the contention that this self-interested bargaining policy does make sense for *any particular group.* Recent research dealing with the influence of trade unions on wages suggests that the existence of organized labor does not change the national distribution of income between workers and owners through collective bargaining, but it may improve the wage situation of one group of workers relative to others. (As will be noted later, it has been argued, however, that aggressive unionism increases national wealth—and thereby workers' incomes—in absolute terms by creating constant pressure on employers to mechanize and increase productivity so as to readjust any imbalances created by increases in labor costs.) Hence the narrow self-interested policies traditionally pursued by many American unions would seem to be warranted if the objective of unionism is to secure as much as possible for the members of the given union. This is most likely to be its objective if the union movement reflects the values of achievement and individualism.

Conversely, however, there seems to be evidence that government can redistribute income among the classes though welfare, tax, and spending policies. Thus, if the labor movement seeks to improve the situation of an entire class, a goal inherent in the economic conflicts which emerged in the previously aristocratic societies, a policy of concentrating on political action rather than trade union militancy is warranted.

Large Wage Differentials

The approval of the pursuit of self-interest within the American labor movement may also help to account for the fact that wage differentials between skilled and unskilled workers are larger in America than in the other nations. A study of such differentials in six countries indicates that in France, Germany, Italy, the Netherlands, and Norway, "skill differentials are rather narrow, compared, say, with United States averages." And: "Differences in wages between unskilled and skilled jobs in Swedish industry are generally much less than in America. For example, the head machine operator in an American paper mill will earn at least 50 per cent more than the lowest paid worker in the mill. In Sweden the difference is less than 20 per cent."

There are many factors related to variations in wage differentials, but it seems possible that variations in basic values may play a role. Sturmthal points this out:

> Undoubtedly also the notions of what are proper differentials . . . vary a good deal on both sides of the Atlantic. The absence of feudal concepts of the place in society to which a worker may properly aspire may have played a part in allowing the larger wage differentials to arise in the United States, just as the heritage of the feudal concepts may have helped maintain the highly compressed wage structure in Europe.

The very insistence on the "formal" equality of all people in the United States places a higher value on income and conspicuous consumption than in societies in which status and occupation are closely linked. Although comparative studies of occupational status indicate that occupations tend to rank at roughly the same level in all industrial societies, occupation seems to be less important than sheer income as a determinant of status in the United States, as compared with some European nations. Two surveys made at about the same time in the United States and Germany suggest this interpretation (see Table I). Although the differences in results may reflect the variations in the questions that were asked, it seems likely that both surveys touched to some extent on the same basic issue: the relative weight given to occupational prestige as compared with the size of income. In both countries those who had higher status (i.e., those who were either better educated or who occupied a white-collar position) were more likely than those of lower status to favor white-collar status, even if it meant lower income than that obtained by a skilled worker. But the important result was that the majority of the American respondents, even among the college graduates, preferred the higher paid, lower status job; on the other hand, the majority of the German respondents ranked the lower paid, white-collar job higher.

TABLE I Preference Percentages for White-Collar Status and Low Income or for Manual Position and High Income in Germany and the United States

UNITED STATES—1951

"Which of these two jobs would you personally prefer a son of yours to take, assuming he is equally qualified: a skilled worker's job at $100 a week, or a white-collar desk job at $75 a week?"

Answer	Total Sample	Years of Education			
		0–8	9–12	13–15	16
White collar	28	22	31	34	42
Skilled laborer	69	72	67	65	52
Don't know	3	6	2	1	6
Total	100.0	100.0	100.0	100.0	100.0
Number interviewed	(658)	(287)	(257)	(62)	(52)

GERMANY—1952

"Who do you think receives more prestige from the population in general: a bookkeeper who earn 300 marks a month, or a foundry worker who brings home 450 marks a month?"

Answer	Total Sample	Manual Worker Respondents Only
The bookkeeper	58	56
The foundry worker	24	28
Don't know	18	16
Total	100.0	100.0

A report on a similar study in another European country, this time a Communist one, Poland, suggests that in that country, as in Germany, white-collar status is given more weight than income. This study, which was apparently more like the American than the German in its approach, indicates that "passage of the better paid skilled manual workers to the position of the slightly lower paid white-collar workers . . . in the majority of cases is looked on as a promotion . . . [although] from the point of view of the new criteria of prestige, this should not be considered a promotion."

Assuming, therefore, that higher occupational status is more of an incentive in countries with relatively formalized status systems than in countries stressing equalitarian behavioral norms, there should be less need in the first group of societies to magnify economic incentives in order to motivate people to prepare for positions requiring long periods of training. As Sturmthal has put it, "incentives that are necessary in one country to produce a certain supply of highly skilled labor may be excessive in another country or *vice versa*. This may be the result of different non-economic compensations offered to the higher skills—status and prestige —or simply of different 'styles of life' in which lesser financial rewards are sufficient to bring about the desired result."

Differences in behavior of organized labor from country to country seem to reflect in some measure variations in the differentials that are considered morally appropriate. Thus, in the United States, for individuals or groups of individuals to seek to better themselves at the expense of others tends to be encouraged by the dominant achievement orientation. In the past few years, several industrial unions formed by the CIO have had difficulty with skilled workers among their membership who have insisted that the wage differentials be widened. In New York, the most highly skilled groups employed on the city's transportation system tried to break away from the Transport Workers' Union to form separate craft unions. A strike called for this purpose failed, but this relatively old industrial union made important concessions to its skilled workers. In the United Automobile Workers the skilled crafts have been allowed to form separate councils within the union and have forced the union to press their demand for greater differentials. In some old craft unions which accepted unskilled and semi-skilled workers, the latter were often given second-class membership, i.e., no voting rights, to prevent them from inhibiting the bargaining strategy of the skilled group.

In much of Europe, on the other hand, the norms implicit in socialist and working-class ideology have made such behavior difficult. The Swedish labor movement for many years made a reduction of differentials one of its aims. Clark Kerr notes that in Germany one of the forces which explains the greater emphasis on wage equality has been "Socialist theories of standardizing pay. . . ." In Italy after World War II, "for political reasons and under the pressure of left-wing parties, the general trend was in favor of raising as much as possible the wages paid to common laborers. . . ." The Norwegian labor movement followed for many years the policy of "wages solidarity," i.e., the reduction of differentials.

In recent years, under pressure from their skilled members and on the advice of various economists who are disturbed by the possible effects on efficiency of narrow differentials for large variations in skills, many of the European labor movements have formally dropped their insistence on narrowing the gap, and some even advocate widening it. As far as the labor economists can judge, the skill differentials, which began dropping in most countries in the late 1930's and continued falling until around 1952, have been rising slightly since then. For socialists, however, to avowedly seek to benefit a more well-to-do group at the expense of the poorer one would seem to violate essential values.[5] And the greater centralization of the union movement in most of these European countries requires that such a wage policy be an explicit national one, rather than one simply reflecting adjustments to immediate pressures.

The general behavior of American unions in perpetuating wide differentials is congruent with the assumption that Americans remain more narrowly self-interested and that the more powerful groups of workers are able to maintain or occasionally even improve a relatively privileged position at the expense of the less powerful, usually less organized, and less skilled workers.[6]

[5] There has, of course, been tension between the skilled and unskilled sections of the labor movement over such issues in most countries. The point here, as in the other comparisons, is always a relative rather than an absolute one. Denmark, for example, represents an extreme case of such internecine warfare. The Laborers Union, the union of the unskilled, which contains almost 40 per cent of all organized workers in the country, has had bitter battles with the craft unions over wage systems. However, as Walter Galenson notes, "Acceptance of socialism by Danish workers by no means eliminated or even dampened internecine strife when important economic interests were involved, but it did contribute to prevention of the breaches of labor solidarity sometimes witnessed in American rival union warfare." And in the 1930's, the Danish Federation of Labor adopted "the so-called 'solidaristic' wage policy, whereby lower paid workers were to receive extra wage concessions. . . ."

[6] Skill and organized collective bargaining power do not necessarily go together. Among the less skilled groups which have powerful unions are the coal miners, the truck drivers, and the West Coast longshoremen. It may also be suggested that one further reason for widespread skill differentials in the United States has been the constant addition of immigrants, most recently Negroes and Puerto Ricans, to the lower occupational strata. Such sources of migration may involve downward pressure on the wages of the unskilled.

SOCIETAL VALUES AND UNION LEADERSHIP

Any effort to account for the ways in which American unionism differs from unionism in northern Europe and Australasia necessarily must deal with the behavior of the leaders. As recent congressional investigations and journalistic exposés have made manifest, union officials in this country receive higher salaries, are more wont to engage in practices which violate conventional morality, and show a lesser regard for the mechanisms of democratic procedure than leaders in the other nations discussed here.

Union Leaders' Job Orientation, Salaries, and Entrenched Positions

The concept of "business unionism," the dominant ideology of the American labor movement which perceives unions as fighting for more money rather than for any program of social reconstruction, has important consequences in encouraging union leaders to view themselves as bound by the same standards as profit-oriented businessmen.

Usually the leaders of social movements are expected to have a "calling," to feel moved by a moral ethic toward serving certain major social values. In the early days of many American unions, when they were weak, often illegitimate, and could yield few rewards in the form of status, power, or income, their leaders did adhere to some such larger ideology, often a variant of socialism. This ideology prescribed certain standards of ethical behavior and a certain style of life. But as American union leaders shifted from social or socialist unionism to business unionism, they also changed their values and standards of comparisons. To a considerable extent, those unions which have retained important aspects of socialist values, such as the United Automobile Workers or the International Ladies Garment Workers Union, are precisely the unions whose leaders, even with great power, still insist upon relatively low officer salaries and show great concern over problems of corruption and civil liberties.[7] To the extent that union office has changed from a "calling" to a "career" as unions have aged and ideology has declined, to that extent have leaders lost their inhibitions about comparing themselves with businessmen or widening the discrepancy between their salaries and those of their members.

[7] The two unions which have established external boards to review appeals from members who feel that they have been deprived of their rights by union officers are the United Automobile Workers and the Upholsterers International Union. Both organizations are still led by men who show various signs of having retained parts of their early socialist beliefs.

The emphasis on pecuniary success, combined with the absence of the kind of class consciousness characteristic of more aristocratic societies, has thus served to motivate workers to use the labor movement itself as an avenue to financial and status gain. The high incomes which many union leaders receive represent their adaptation to the norm of "getting ahead." As long as a union leader has the reputation for "delivering the goods" to his members, they seem willing to allow him a high salary and sometimes the rights to engage in private business, or even to be corrupt.

The greater perquisites attached to high union office in America, a seeming consequence of pressure inherent in the achievement-equalitarianism syndrome, may also account for the fact that American union leaders have formally institutionalized dictatorial mechanisms which prevent the possibility of their being defeated for re-election. Although trade-union leaders in all countries have achieved a great deal by moving up from the machine or bench to the union office, this shift has nowhere meant as much in terms of money and consequent style of life as in the United States. Most high status positions carry with them some security of tenure, but political positions in democratic societies are insecure by definition. Politicians in most countries may move from electoral defeat to highly paid positions in private industry or the professions, but union leaders customarily cannot do so. This means, as I have noted elsewhere, that they are under considerable pressure to find means to protect their source of status. Thus the greater the gap between the rewards of union leadership and of those jobs from which the leader came and to which he might return on defeat, the greater the pressure to eliminate democratic rights. Within the American labor movement itself those unions in which the gap between leaders and rank and file is narrow in income or in status seem to be much more democratic than those in which the gap is great. Among the unions which fall in this former category are Actors' Equity, the American Newspaper Guild, and the International Typographical Union. Thus the very forces which press for higher rewards of various types for American labor leaders also support and encourage greater restrictions on democratic politics in the unions.

It may also be argued that in societies in which deferential values are strong, union leaders may maintain an oligarchic structure with less strain than is possible in America. And as I stated in an earlier essay:

> Given the assumption that leaders in both [continents] would seek to make their tenure secure, we would expect that American labor leaders would be under greater pressure to formalize dictatorial mechanisms so as to prevent the possibility of their being overthrown. Or, to put it another way, since the values inherent in American society operate to make American union officers more vulnerable than, say, their German

counterparts, they would be obliged to act more vigorously and decisively and dictatorially to stabilize their status.

Some evidence that relatively elite societies are more willing to give tenure to union leaders may be found in Great Britain and Sweden, where the principal officers of many national unions are formally chosen for life. Although similar commitments are much less common elsewhere, actual opposition to the re-election of national leaders is almost non-existent among most European unions. Lower level leaders and convention delegates may and often do oppose top leadership policies, but such opposition—and even successful efforts to change policies by convention vote—are rarely linked to an effort to replace the high-ranking officers.

The logic of the argument presented here is similar to that made by many foreign analysts of American stratification, who have suggested that precisely because of the antagonism to aristocratic values in the United States, upper-class Americans—as contrasted with upper-class Europeans—are more likely to be concerned with the social origins and social backgrounds for those with whom they associate at play, in clubs, in school, and so forth. Insecurity stemming from an equalitarian democracy's denial of permanent status, calls forth defensive reactions on the part of those who would preserve their positions.

The Large Number and Proportion of Paid Union Officials

Perhaps even more important in affecting the varying quality of the internal political life of American and European unions is the difference in the sheer number and proportion of full-time officers. A recent ILO mission of European labor authorities studying American unions was impressed by "the number of paid posts at all levels of union organization," as contrasted with the much lower number in Europe. The most recent available data for various countries are reported in Table II. These indi-

TABLE II   Numbers and Proportions of Full-Time Union Officers in Various Countries

Country	Total union membership	Total number full-time officers	Approximate ratio of officers to members
United States	18,000,000	60,000	1:300
Australia	2,400,000	2,500–2,750	1:900
Great Britain	8,000,000	4,000	1:2,000
Sweden	1,500,000	900	1:1,700
Norway	500,000	240	1:2,200
Denmark	775,000	1,000	1:775

cate one officer for every 300 union members in the United States, while three of the northern European movements, those of Britain, Norway, and Sweden, have one officer for every 1,700 to 2,200 members.

In Britain, Norway, Sweden, Belgium, and many other European countries, lay union officers and committees, i.e., men working full time at their regular occupations while voluntarily performing union duties, carry out many of the tasks which are performed by full-time union executives and staff men in the United States. National officers clearly cannot have the same degree of control over lay subordinates which they have over paid officers whose tenure in, or advancement up, the union hierarchy usually depends on being in the good graces of the top leaders. To some degree, those who serve as unpaid officers must be men with a sense of mission, who view the movements as something more than an "insurance policy" for personal success, and who expect their paid officers to adhere to the values of a social movement. Such lay leaders will clearly remain relatively close in social position and values to the rank and file. In large measure, the perpetuation of serious political debate within union movements such as the British, the Norwegian, or the Belgian reflects the fact that many lay leaders are drawn from the ranks of the more idealistic and politically motivated of the membership and are not on a union career ladder.

In the United States, the large number of paid officials at all levels often means the union conventions are to a considerable extent meetings of the full-time local, district, and national leaders. Such meetings are much less likely to create trouble for the national officers than are meetings composed largely of men who are deeply involved in union matters, but who continue to work at their trade. The British Amalgamated Engineering Union, one of the largest in the country, has a lay national committee of fifty-two members which is authorized to give the full-time executive council "instructions for the ensuing year"; and B. C. Roberts comments that this "is precisely what it does, and it enforces its constitutional authority on a not always readily compliant executive council . . . [which] is not infrequently prevented from pursuing a wise policy by the powerful national committee." In most British unions, "lay status, that is, holding of no full-time office in the union, and non-membership on the executive council is generally necessary" to be a delegate to a national convention.

Extensive lay involvement in union affairs does not, of course, prevent the paid officials from effectively controlling policy on most matters most of the time. An analysis of the voting on resolutions at nine British conventions during 1950–1952 indicated that the leaders were defeated on only 31 occasions out of 428 conference votes. But in countries in which most of the secondary leadership are men who work at their trade, national executives are subject to more pressure to conform to conventional norms of morality and due process than when the lower echelons are paid union officers.[8] And even though British top union officers, for example, usually remain in office as long as do the entrenched heads of American organizations, the practice of lay participation on all levels permits a greater part in decision-making by the rank-and-file activists, who become unpaid officers, committeemen, and delegates to conventions. Thus Hugh Clegg points to the fact that a major policy of the British unions, the decision made in 1948 to cooperate with the Labor Government's wage restraint policy, was reversed in 1950 "through the gradual process of branch votes and conference decisions in the individual unions. This took place without the wholesale replacement of trade-union executives and officers by opposition leaders. . . ."

The fact that union activists, in the form of lay officers and committeemen, have much more influence over the policy of national unions in Britain than in America does not necessarily mean that the British unions more accurately reflect the sentiment of their general membership. The activists are much more likely to be radical than either the rank-and-file membership as a whole or the national leadership. This was clearly shown in the case of the 1960 debate over unilateral disarmament. A national opinion survey conducted in September 1960, shortly before the Labor Party conference, reported that only 16 per cent of trade-union members favored the proposal that Britain unilaterally give up its nuclear weapons, the very policy which was backed by a majority of the delegates representing the trade unions; 83 per cent of rank-and-file union members expressed the opinion that Britain should retain such weapons until other powers agreed to disarm.

Although it is relatively easy to suggest some of the effects of the variation in the proportion of full-time officers on trade-union government and behavior, it is much more difficult to explain the source of the variation. Some have suggested that it reflects differences in the income of labor organizations in Europe and America. While this factor undoubtedly plays a role (though Swedish unions are quite well-to-do),

[8] Another interesting consequence of a high proportion of paid officials has been suggested by John Dunlop, in discussing the causes of jurisdictional disputes in the building trades unions in the United States. "The large number of paid union officials at the local level with direct supervision over members at job sites is a feature . . . of workers' organizations in the United States system. 'Professionals' are available to appear at job sites to draw fine lines of jurisdiction. National and local union rivalries are expressed at the work place because the machinery and manpower to express them on the job is available. In other countries . . . few full-time professionals are available to police the rules. . . . Left to themselves on the job site, the workers would engage in fewer and less severe disputes."

the fact remains that American unions began the practice of employing full-time officers and staff members when many of the unions were weak and impoverished. In discussing the American labor movement, the Swedish sociologist and economist Gunnar Myrdal points out that the foreign observer "is struck by the importance played by salaried 'organizers' and the relative unimportance of, or often the lack of, a spontaneous drive from the workers themselves." He suggests that this phenomenon reflects the general "passivity of the masses in America [which] is, of course, a product of the nation's history." Specifically, immigration produced cultural fragmentation and prevented strong interest-group identification, while a very high rate of social mobility drained the working class of its potential leaders.

Although the factors which Myrdal cites may account in part for the relatively low level of "class consciousness" among American workers, they do not explain the apparent willingness from a very early period in trade-union history to pay leaders full-time salaries. As a further factor contributing to this policy, it may be suggested that inherent in the ideology of an equalitarian society like ours, as contrasted with those of countries like Britain and Sweden in which aristocratic values remain significant, has been the principle that a man should be paid for his work. The conception that public or social service is performed best when a leader is not paid, or is paid an honorarium, is basically an aristocratic value linked to the concept of *noblesse oblige.* In Britain, for example, recent parliamentary discussions concerning the salaries of Members of Parliament have explicitly assumed that M.P.'s should not be paid well, because it would be bad if men were attracted to a parliamentary career in order to better themselves economically. The inhibitions against employing a large number of officials permeate most voluntary associations in the European nations and reflect the historic assumption that such activities should be the "charities" of the privileged classes. The absence of a model of *noblesse oblige* in an equalitarian society fostered the American belief that such voluntary associations, whether they be the "March of Dimes," social work agencies, or trade unions, should be staffed by men who are paid to do the job. In a sense, therefore, it may be argued that the very emphasis on equalitarianism in America has given rise to the large salaried bureaucracies which permeate voluntary organizations.

In presenting this hypothesis, I do not mean to suggest that historic differences in ultimate values themselves account for the perpetuation and extension of the varying patterns down to the present. Rather, the different values in Europe and America helped to initiate differing early models of behavior, which became institutionalized within varying social structures. The European practice fostered—and in turn has been sus-

tained by—the ideologies, mainly socialist, which the various labor movements adopted. Conversely, in the United States the establishment of the
union career ladder made union leaders receptive to incorporating the
society's achievement norms into the ideology and practice of the movement, and these norms supported further extension of the practice of
maintaining a large and well-paid bureaucracy and leadership core.

THE AMERICAN POLITICAL SYSTEM AND
THE UNION MOVEMENT

The difference between the American labor movement and those in
other modern industrial countries cannot be attributed solely to the direct
effect of American values on its ideology. The greater authority and
power centered in the hands of American national union presidents, as
compared with European leaders,[9] may also be viewed as an outgrowth
of the role of the executive and of federalism in American politics.

As a result of its history and size, the United States has adopted two
distinct political institutions, the presidential system and the federal system. Our principal elections at the national, state, and local levels are for
one man—the president, governor, or mayor. Government is largely
viewed as the government of the man who holds the key executive office.
His cabinet is responsible to him, not to his party nor to parliamentary
colleagues. Hence there is an emphasis on personality and a relative de-
emphasis of party or principles. These factors, which have become nor-
mative elements in the political sphere, undoubtedly affect the way in
which other institutions, such as unions, operate.

The federal system, with its relatively strong local government institutions, has also affected the logic and organization of trade unions, since
many of them are involved in various kinds of relations with the centers
of political power. If political power for certain major purposes rests on
the level of the municipality, this means that unions too must be able to
deal with local officials. But probably at least as important as this structural parallelism is the fact that federalism and local self-government have
facilitated the maintenance of strong norms of local and regional solidarity and consciousness of difference from other parts of the nation. Business
power, also, is comparatively decentralized in the United States. The norms
support the institutionalization of competition; this is reflected in the
early passage of anti-trust laws and other legislation against unfair re-

---

[9] The English labor authority B. C. Roberts has commented, "Once elected, the
power of an American union president generally far exceeds that of any officer of
British or Scandinavian unions."

straint of trade. Unions have to deal not only with local political power but with local business power as well. And business groups in various parts of the country often follow different strategies.[10]

The decentralization of authority may be related to other aspects of union behavior discussed earlier. There are fewer organizational restrictions on union militancy when authority is decentralized. National agreements require centralization of union authority and inhibit locally called strikes. Hence American union militancy may be partly a reflection of the prevalence of local agreements, which, as we have seen, may be regarded as an indirect consequence of the overreaching value system.

The militancy of American unions, which has been derived from attributes and consequences of these basic values, may in turn be one of the major factors contributing to the pattern of innovation which characterizes the economy. The editors of the London *Economist* have suggested that the historic propensity of American unions to demand "more" forces employers to find ways to resolve their dilemma by improving productivity. "Thus, there is generated a constant force pushing the employer into installing more labor-saving equipment, into reducing costs in other directions." European unions with their involvement in making national contracts and with their regard for the over-all needs of the polity and economy—concerns which seem in some measures to stem from their political commitments—are less inclined to make "irresponsible" demands or to insist on policies which will adversely affect a sizable part of an industry. Decentralized collective bargaining is in part an *outgrowth* of a dynamic economy in which different portions are advancing at varying rates, and in part a *cause* of that very dynamism.

Decentralization of power also facilitates corruption. Corruption in American unions and other institutions is more prevalent on the local than on the national level. Where lower level officials such as union business agents or municipal inspectors deal directly with businessmen, the possibilities of undetected corruption are much greater than they are in relations among the heads of major organizations.

Political decentralization and strong local governments, as Tocqueville noted well over a century ago, strongly reinforce the norms of individualism. Americans are encouraged to press for their objectives through

[10] The ILO Mission points out in the conclusion of its report: "Much has been said in this report about the different conditions for trade union activity which are found in different parts of the country. . . . The general public attitude towards trade unions may vary from one state, city or locality to another. Relations with the employers vary in the same way. The relations between the unions and a company may not be the same in all the company's plants in different areas. Unions which are accepted in certain industries in some parts of the country may be opposed in the same industries in other parts."

individual or organized group action, not to accept their lot or to hope for remedy from an established upper class or a strong central government. Over time, of course, changes in technology and the nature of social problems have led to increasing centralization of power within government, business, and labor. But it still remains true that, on a comparative scale, American institutions remain decentralized and local units retain considerable autonomy. Hence one has here another example of inter-related supports and consequences of the dominant value system.

Within the labor movement, the emphasis on strong local organizations has, in turn, facilitated the creation of the large numbers of full-time union positions referred to earlier. Thus in its decentralization, as in its conservative politics and militant strike tactics, the American union may be viewed as an outgrowth of the American social and American value system.

Knights of Labor Versus American Federation of Labor

GERALD N. GROB

From the earliest labor activity at the begining of the nineteenth century, the American movement evinced two tendencies—one intent on total reform of the economic order, the other limited to job improvement within the existing system. In the formative years, no distinct line had divided reform and economic unionism; men and organizations shifted back and forth, with the reform tendency normally dominating in times of economic adversity. But as the institutional forms of trade unionism stabilized and the industrial system matured, the inherent incompatability between economic and reform unionism became increasingly acute. During the 1880s, the labor movement made its choice. In this classic modern account, Gerald N. Grob analyzes the climactic clash between the national trade unions and the Knights of Labor. Other scholars, such as Norman Ware and Selig Perlman, have seen in the Knights the makings of a form of trade unionism alternative to craft organization. Grob, however, defines the issue strictly along the line of reform versus economic unionism. He argues that the Knights of Labor was a reform movement both in structure and ideology, and that it posed a threat that had to be met and defeated by the trade unions.

THE YEAR 1886 WAS DESTINED TO BE A CRUCIAL ONE IN THE history of the American labor movement. The eight-hour crusade, the numerous strikes, the Haymarket bomb, the entrance of workingmen into the political arena at the state and national levels, and the mushroom growth of labor organizations all contributed to the agitation and excitement of the year. Yet the importance of these events was over-

From Gerald N. Grob, "The Knights of Labor and the Trade Unions, 1878–1886," *The Journal of Economic History,* XVIII (June, 1958), pp. 176–192. Reprinted by permission of the publisher. Footnotes have been omitted except where they amplify the text.

shadowed by a development that was to have such far-reaching implications that it would determine the future of the labor movement for the succeeding half century. That development was the declaration of war by the trade unions against the reform unionism of the Knights of Labor.

The struggle between the Knights and the other unions represented a clash of two fundamentally opposing ideologies. The Knights of Labor, on the one hand, grew out of the reform and humanitarian movements of ante-bellum America, and was the direct descendent, through the National Labor Union, of the labor reform tradition of the Jacksonian era. Banking on the leveling influence of technological change, its leaders sought to organize the entire producing class into a single irresistible coalition that would work toward the abolition of the wage system and the establishment of a new society. "We do not believe," a high official of the Knights remarked, "that the emancipation of labor will come with increased wages and a reduction in the hours of labor; we must go deeper than that, and this matter will not be settled until the wage system is abolished." The leaders of the Knights therefore emphasized education and co-operation, and they bitterly opposed their constituents' participation in such affairs as the Southwest and stockyard strikes in 1886, as well as the very popular eight-hour movement of that same year.

The reform ideology of the Knights, in turn, had an important impact upon the development of its structure, which followed a heterogeneous rather than a homogeneous pattern. Minimizing the utility of organization along trade lines, the Order emphasized instead the grouping of all workers, regardless of craft, into a single body. Highest priority therefore was given to the mixed local assembly, which included all workers irrespective of their trade or degree of skill. Neither a trade, plant, nor industrial union, the mixed assembly could never be more than a study or debating group. Including many diverse elements (even employers), it could not adapt itself to meet the problems of a specific industry or trade. The mixed assembly might agitate for reform or participate in politics, but it could never become the collective bargaining representative of its members.

Given the predominance of the mixed over the trade local, the structure of the Knights inevitably developed along geographical rather than jurisdictional lines, and the district assembly, which included mixed as well as trade locals, became the most characteristic form of organization. The highest governmental body of the Knights—the General Assembly—was not intended as a medium for collective bargaining. Indeed, its very inclusiveness precluded such a possibility.

The trade unions, on the other hand, rejected the broad reform goals of the Knights, emphasizing instead higher wages, shorter hours, and job control. Such objectives were clearly incompatible with an organizational structure such as that developed by the Knights. Eschewing the multitrade local that had been so prevalent during the 1860's and was being perpetuated by the Order, the trade unions began to stress the craft-industrial form of organization both at the local and national levels. A relative scarcity of labor, together with a rapidly expanding economy, had created a favorable environment for the trade unions. Gambling on the hope that the rise of a national market made organization along trade rather than geographical lines more effective, union leaders chose to concentrate upon the task of organizing the workers along trade lines into unions designed for collective bargaining rather than social reform.

Therefore, given the inherent differences in ideology and structure, the conflict between the Knights and the trade unions was, if not inevitable, certainly not an unexpected or surprising development. Undoubtedly the antagonistic personalities of partisans on both sides hastened an open rift. Yet the hostilities between the Knights and the trade unions cannot be explained solely in terms of personalities, for the conflict was not simply a struggle for power between two rivals. It was a clash between two fundamentally different ideologies—with the future of the labor movement at stake.

I

The contest between trade unionists and reformers for control of the labor movement developed on two planes. Commencing first as an internal struggle within the Knights, it eventually expanded and soon involved the national unions. Within the Knights the struggle revolved around the unresolved question as to which form of organization best met working-class necessities. On the surface the issue of mixed versus trade locals was simply a structural problem. In reality, however, the differences between the two forms indicated the existence of a fundamental cleavage in ultimate objectives, for the mixed assembly could be utilized only for reform or political purposes, while the trade assembly was generally a collective bargaining organization.

Although the national leadership of the Knights regarded the mixed assembly as the ideal type of unit, a large proportion of its local assemblies were trade rather than mixed. The first local, composed of garment cutters, was strictly craft, and remained so to the end. Most of the other locals that followed were also trade assemblies. On January 1, 1882, according to the *Journal of United Labor,* there were 27 working districts and over 400 local assemblies. Of the latter, 318 were trade and only 116 were mixed. Thirteen additional districts, not functioning, had 53 trade and 87 mixed locals, attesting to the relative instability of the mixed form of organization. Of the 135 locals attached directly to the General Assembly, 67 were trade and 68 were mixed.

Despite the wide latitude given them to organize trade local assemblies, the trade element within the Knights nevertheless found it difficult to function efficiently. Local trade assemblies, no matter how inclusive in their particular area, were often ineffective when operating in a market that was regional or national rather than local in character. So long as employers could find a ready supply of nonunion labor elsewhere, efforts at collective bargaining by locals would be ineffective. The only solution lay in national organization, and the trade exponents within the Knights pressed for national and regional trade districts that would transcend the limited geographical area normally encompassed by the local or district assembly.

The General Assembly, therefore, meeting in January 1879, authorized the establishment of autonomous national trade districts within the framework of the Knights. But only nine months later the Assembly completely reversed itself by declaring that trade locals were "contrary to the spirit and genius of the Order," and it returned exclusive jurisdiction over all locals to the district assembly of their area.

In December 1881, however, the Federation of Organized Trades and Labor Unions, predecessor of the American Federation of Labor (A.F. of L.), held its first convention. Of the 107 delegates present, no less than 50 came from the Knights.

The following September the General Assembly heard the secretary of the Knights warn that trade sentiment was growing rapidly. "Many Trades Unions have also written me," he remarked, "stating that they were seriously meditating the propriety of coming over to us in a body, freely expressing the opinion that their proper place was in our Order." To prevent any mass exodus from the Order to the rival Federation, and also to recruit members from the trade unions, the General Assembly enacted legislation authorizing and encouraging the formation of national and regional trade districts. This move was reaffirmed and even extended at the meetings of the General Assembly in 1884 and 1886.

While permissible, at least in theory, the establishment of trade districts was not a simple matter. The basic philosophy of the Knights militated against organization along craft lines, and the establishment of autonomous trade units within the framework of the Order aroused strong opposition. "I do not favor the establishment of any more National Trade Districts," Terence V. Powderly, head of the Knights from 1879 to 1893, told the General Assembly in 1885, "they are a step backward." Other reform unionists, echoing Powderly's sentiments, charged that trade districts violated the fundamental principles of the Knights. Holding tenaciously to their reform concepts, the leaders of the Knights were insistent in their demands that organization should not proceed along trade lines.

Applicants for trade districts therefore could not always be certain that charters would be granted them, even though they had met all the formal requirements. In some cases charters were granted without any questions. Window Glass Workers' Local Assembly (L.A.) 300 was chartered as a national trade district at a time when such districts were contrary to the laws of the Knights, and the telegraphers were organized nationally in 1882 as District Assembly (D.A.) 45. For a while these two were the only national districts, although before 1886 there were two district assemblies composed of miners, five of shoemakers, three of railroad employees, and one each of printers, plumbers, leather workers, government employees, and streetcar employees. Between 1883 and 1885 the General Assembly went on record as favoring the establishment of trade districts of shoemakers, plate-glass workers, and plumbers. On the other hand, after sanctioning the formation of builders' districts in 1882, it refused the following year to permit these districts to be represented on the General Executive Board. Even while passing legislation authorizing trade districts, the General Assembly refused to allow woodworkers, cigarmakers, and carpenters to organize trade districts. Furthermore, it passed a resolution stating that no charter for a trade district would be granted unless the applicants could demonstrate to the satisfaction of the General Executive Board that the craft could not be effectively organized under the system of mixed or territorial districts. The attitude of the board, however, was often conditioned by the antitrade unionism of its officers. In 1886, for example, it refused to sanction the request of five building trade locals that they be permitted to withdraw from D.A. 66 and organize their own district. At the same time it empowered a New Hampshire local to change from a trade to a mixed assembly.

Trade units, generally speaking, were authorized usually in efforts to attract workers to join the Knights. Thus the International Trunkmakers Union came into the Order as a trade district. Once inside, however, workers found it considerably more difficult to secure trade charters. After affiliating in 1882, to cite one case, the plumbers later left the Knights when they encountered difficulty in obtaining a charter for a national trade district, and they established the International Association of Journeymen Plumbers, Steam Fitters, and Gas Fitters.

The hostility of the national leadership of the Knights was not the sole obstacle to the formation of trade units. Mixed and territorial districts, which were first in the field and were already established as functioning organizations, were also antagonistic toward trade districts. If the latter were formed, not only would a mixed district suffer a loss of membership to a trade district, but it would also surrender its absolute jurisdiction over a given territorial area, since the autonomous trade district would exercise control over the entire craft in that area.

The General Assembly and the General Executive Board often supported the mixed and territorial districts in disputes with trade districts. Frequently the district's consent was a prerequisite to secession and the establishment of a trade district. This consent was not easily obtained. In 1886 D.A. 30 of Massachusetts turned down an application by four of its locals for permission to withdraw and form a national trade assembly of rubber workers. While the General Assembly supported a district court decision that members of trade locals could not be compelled to join mixed locals, the General Executive Board refused to force trade members of mixed locals to transfer to trade assemblies.

Even after obtaining a charter, trade districts encountered difficulties with the mixed district in their areas. Dual jurisdiction often led to friction, though in theory the system of mixed and trade districts appeared perfectly harmonious and compatible. For example, D.A. 64 of New York City, composed of workers in the printing and publishing business, became embroiled in a rivalry with D.A. 49 (mixed). In 1883 D.A. 64 failed to get exclusive jurisdiction over all workers in the trade. Soon afterward D.A. 49 charged that the printers were accepting locals not of their trade, and that these locals had also withdrawn from D.A. 49 without permission. An investigation by the secretary of the General Executive Board disclosed that D.A. 64 had been initiating lithographers, typefounders, pressmen, and feeders in order to strengthen itself as a bargaining unit, and that it had not engaged in raiding forays against D.A. 49. Although the Board upheld D.A. 64, the decision did not resolve the rivalry, and the two districts continued their feud.

With the single exception of L.A. 300, trade districts did not enjoy any appreciable measure of success between 1878 and 1885. The far-reaching reform goals of the Knights and its structural inclusiveness left the advocates of trade organization in the position of a perpetual minority. The expansion of the Knights into the more sparsely populated regions of the South and West, moreover, further diminished trade influence, since the mixed assembly was dominant in rural areas. Lacking a majority, the trade members were unable to establish a central strike fund or concentrate on collective bargaining, and they found that their immediate goals were being subordinated to and sacrificed for more utopian objectives.

II

The struggle between trade unionists and reformers within the Knights, however, was completely overshadowed by the rupture of relations in

1886 between the Knights and the national unions. The latter, stronger and more cohesive than the trade districts of the Order, were better able to take the lead in the conflict between reform and trade unionism. Disillusioned with labor reformism, the trade unions acted upon the premise that the traditional programs of the past were no longer suitable to the changing environment, and they led the assault against the Knights of Labor in 1886.

During the early 1880's, however, it was by no means evident that the Knights and the national unions were predestined to clash. The Federation of Organized Trades and Labor Unions permitted district assemblies of the Knights to be represented at its annual conventions, and many trade union leaders also belonged to the Order. Local unions and assemblies often co-operated in joint boycotts, and expressions of friendliness by the national unions toward Powderly and other officials of the Knights were not uncommon. The International Typographical Union expressed appreciation in 1882 for the aid given it by the Knights in a number of cities, and then went on to adopt resolutions recommending co-operation with other labor organizations and permitting its members to join any body that would further the interests of the craft in their particular locality. In other words, the national unions regarded the Knights as a valuable economic ally.

In turn, the Knights vehemently denied having any hostile designs upon the trade unions, and in a number of prominent cases before 1885 it acted accordingly. Nevertheless, with its structural inclusiveness and reform ideology, it was perhaps inevitable that the Order, in its efforts to bring all workingmen into a single organization, would undercut trade union organizational efforts. Thus the General Assembly authorized a committee in 1883 to confer with union representatives in the hope of incorporating all the trade unions within the Knights.

In the absence of any national or international union, the absorption of local unions by the Knights in the form of trade assemblies created no friction. Indeed, isolated local unions were eager to affiliate with such a powerful national organization. By 1886, therefore, the Knights claimed nearly eleven hundred local assemblies, many of which undoubtedly represented local trade unions having no parent national union.

When, however, the Knights began to organize workingmen in trades already having national organizations, friction was quick to arise. The trouble that followed the Order's expansion into the realm of the trade unions was not simply a jurisdictional rivalry between similar organizations. As discussed above, the Order and the national unions had opposing conceptions of the legitimate functions of the labor movement, which in turn had led to different structural forms. The expansion of the Order's mixed units thus served to undermine the economic functions of the trade unions, since the heterogeneous character of the former prevented them from exercising any appreciable degree of economic power. Furthermore, the structural diversity of the Knights caused trouble when its trade assemblies sought to perform tasks that logically fell within the purview of the trade unions. The national unions, moreover, took the position that geographical trade assemblies were inadequate to meet the challenge of a nationalized economy, and in fact were little better than mixed district assemblies. In defense, union officials generally refused to consent to a mutual recognition of working cards, and they demanded that the Knights cease interfering in trade affairs.

The Knights, however, did not heed the warnings of the national unions, and its organizers continued their sporadic work in trades having national unions. "Every week," John Swinton reported in 1885, "Trades Unions are turned into Local Assemblies, or Assemblies are organized out of Trade Unions." As early as 1881 a district leader attempted to capture a typographical union local, and by 1884 there were over forty local assemblies of printers in the Knights. The overzealous activities of the Order's organizers also led to trouble with the Bricklayers and Masons International Union.

The trade unions continuously charged that the Order had accepted scabs and unfair workers. It is probable that the unions greatly exaggerated this grievance, but there is little doubt that the existence of two labor organizations, each purporting to accomplish different ends, created a disciplinary problem. Intraunion disagreements frequently concluded with one party seceding and joining the Order as a local assembly. Thus the trade unions found that the Knights were attracting dissidents who normally might have remained in the union.

Despite the proselytizing activities of the Knights, there was no general conflict with the other unions before July 1885. At this time the membership of the Order was slightly over 100,000, and examples of clashes with the trade unions were generally the exception rather than the rule. When differences did arise, the trade unions often made conciliatory efforts at peaceful adjustment. Thus the convention of the International Typographical Union agreed in 1884 to its president's suggestion that he confer with Powderly in order to iron out existing grievances, although it refused to sanction a proposed amalgamation with the Order.

In only one major case—that involving the Cigar Makers International Union—did the differences between a national union and the Knights erupt in open hostilities before 1886. Historians, placing much emphasis upon this particular conflict, have credited Adolph Strasser and Samuel Gompers, the leaders of the Cigar Makers, with the dual responsibility of helping to precipitate the internecine war between the national unions and the Knights, and then founding the A.F. of L. as a rival national federation.

While the national unions generally supported the Cigar Makers in its struggle with the Knights, it is improbable that sympathy for the Cigar Makers would have led to a fight with the Order. Undoubtedly Strasser and Gompers exerted great efforts to induce the unions to lend them support. The fact is also incontrovertible that both were determined, forceful, and sometimes ruthless men. Nevertheless, their efforts would have been useless unless a solid basis of discontent had already existed. In other words, for the unions to break with the Knights, there must have been more compelling reasons than simply the activities of two individuals.

III

To understand the conflict that split the labor movement, the rapid growth of the Knights after 1885 must be examined. In the twelve months between July 1885 and June 1886 the Order's membership increased from 100,000 to over 700,000. This growth, at least in part, came about at the expense of the other unions. In many cases workers abandoned their trade unions to join the Knights. The Journeymen Tailors National Union found that many of its locals had transferred to the Knights, resulting in a considerable loss of membership. A vice-president of the Amalgamated Association of Iron and Steel Workers complained in 1886 that some sublodges in his area had been disbanded because of inroads by the Order. Further difficulty was caused by overzealous organizers who made determined efforts to transform trade unions into local assemblies. In February 1886 the secretary of the Journeymen Bakers National Union protested against such activities. "We never knew," responded the secretary-treasurer of the Knights, "that the K. of L. was proscribed from bringing into its fold all branches of honorable toil."

The Knights, in other words, had adopted an organizational policy diametrically different from that of the trade unions. The traditional concept of organization held by the A.F. of L. (the representative of the trade unions) required that federal labor unions (local units including workers of all trades having no separate unions of their own) be splintered into separate homogeneous craft units as soon as there were enough workers in that locality to form such bodies. The aim of such a policy was to develop the collective bargaining potentialities of the various trades. The Knights, on the other hand, sought to reverse this strategy and proceed in the opposite direction, and it encouraged the combining of trade units into mixed assemblies, which at most were reform or political units.

Beneath the structural and organizational differences of the two groups, therefore, lay opposing goals.

To what extent did the Knights encroach upon the domain of the trade unions? Peter J. McGuire of the Carpenters claimed that between 150 and 160 trade unions, including the Molders, Boiler-Makers, Bakers, Miners, Typographical, and Granite Cutters, had grievances against the Order. Only in the case of the Bricklayers and Masons International Union, however, is the evidence fairly complete. In response to a survey conducted in the summer of 1886, the union's secretary received eighty-seven replies. Eight locals reported the existence of bricklayers and masons assemblies within their jurisdiction, four claimed the Knights were working for subunion wages, and three asserted the Knights were working longer hours. "But there are a large number of such men scattered throughout the country who belong to mixed assemblies," the secretary reported—and herein lay the union's major grievance. The complaints of the Bricklayers and Masons were echoed by most of the other major national unions.

In general, the national unions were fearful of the Knights for two closely related reasons. The mixed assembly, in the first place, was incompatible with trade union goals. In theory both structural forms could exist side by side, each pursuing its own ends. Thus the mixed assembly could concentrate on reform and politics, while the trade unions could develop their collective bargaining functions. This *modus vivendi,* however, presupposed that workers could belong simultaneously to both trade unions and mixed assemblies. At a time when the labor movement's primary problem was to organize and stay organized, such an assumption was unwarranted, and trade union leaders recognized the mutual hostility of the mixed assembly and trade union.

In the second place, trade union officials opposed the chartering of trade assemblies within the Knights for the reason that these units had proved incapable of developing collective bargaining and other union institutions. Furthermore, the geographical and regional organization of the Knights meant that there was little hope for the mature evolution of the national trade assembly. Since local trade assemblies were often ineffective when operating in an environment marked by a nationalized economy and the geographical mobility of labor, trade union leaders argued that these unions were attempting to perform functions that logically belonged to the national unions, and in the long run tended to undermine the standards of membership and employment that the unions had struggled so fiercely to establish.

By the spring of 1886 relations between the trade unions and the Knights had so deteriorated that a collision appeared imminent. Five prominent unionists therefore called for a meeting of union leaders to arrange a settlement of differences, while at the same time Powderly summoned the General Assembly in a special session to consider, among other things, the troubles with the trade unions. The conference of trade union officials then appointed a committee of five to draw up a plan of settlement. Under the moderating influence of McGuire, who played the leading role, the committee drew up a "treaty," which it submitted to the General Executive Board of the Knights on May 25, 1886.

By the terms of this treaty the Knights would refrain from organizing any trade having a national organization, and also would revoke the charter of any existing trade assembly having a parent union. In the second place, any workers guilty of ignoring trade union wage scales, scabbing, or any other offense against a union, would be ineligible for membership in the Order. Third, any organizer who tampered with or interfered in the internal affairs of trade unions would have his commission revoked. Finally, local and district assemblies were not to interfere while trade unions engaged in strikes or lockouts, and the Knights would not be permitted to issue any label or trade-mark where a national union had already done so.

On the surface it appears surprising that the trade unions, which claimed to represent about 350,000 workers (although their actual membership was about 160,000), would present such a document to an organization having 700,000 members. Yet the treaty was neither a bargaining offer nor a declaration of war. It was rather the logical outcome of the duality that had pervaded the labor movement since the Civil War. Under its terms the labor movement would be divided into two separate and distinct compartments. The Knights of Labor, on the one hand, would continue its efforts to abolish the wage system, reform society, and educate the working class. The national unions, on the other hand, would be left paramount in the economic field, and the Order would no longer be permitted to exercise any control over wages, hours, working conditions, or the process of collective bargaining. In other words, trade unionism and reform unionism had come to a parting of the ways.

In one sense the treaty was an expression of the fear of the skilled workers that they were being subordinated to the interests of the unskilled.[1] Yet the polarization implied in such an interpretation should

[1] Perlman has interpreted the conflict between the Knights and unions largely as one between skilled and unskilled workers. Undoubtedly the skilled workers feared the Knights. The Knights, however, was not necessarily an organization of unskilled workers, as the large number of trade assemblies would indicate. While the unions jealously guarded their autonomy and independence, the conflict that developed in 1886 was more than simply a struggle between the skilled and unskilled, although this aspect was an important element.

not be exaggerated, for it cannot be said that the Knights themselves represented the unskilled workers. The Order was not an industrial union, nor did it emphasize collective bargaining. It was rather a heterogeneous mass that subordinated the economic functions of labor organizations to its primary goal of reforming society. The mixed assembly, while including workers of all trades and callings, was in no sense an industrial union, since it was not organized either by industry or factory. Moreover, the trade unions had never excluded the unskilled from the labor movement; they simply maintained that organization along craft lines was historically correct. "In truth," remarked Gompers, "the trade union is nothing more or less than the organization of wage earners engaged in a given employment, whether skilled or unskilled, for the purpose of attaining the best possible reward, [and] the best attainable conditions for the workers in that trade or calling."

The General Assembly of the Knights, in turn, submitted its own proposals to the union committee. Its terms included protection against unfair workers, a mutual exchange of working cards, and the holding of a joint conference before either organization presented wages and hours demands to employers. Clearly the Assembly's position was in fundamental disagreement with that of the trade unions. The latter had demanded unitary control over the economic field, while the Knights had demanded equal jurisdiction over membership and working standards. Thus neither side evinced willingness to compromise over basic issues.

Although failing to conclude a settlement with the trade unions, the special session of the General Assembly did not close the door to further negotiations. For the time being, therefore, the conflict remained in abeyance. While matters were pending, however, the Knights made a determined effort to end friction by intensifying its campaign to bring the national unions under its control. The national unions, however, recognized that the structure of the Knights was incompatible with trade union objectives, and the policy of the Order was only partially successful. Some of the smaller unions, including the Seamen's Benevolent Union, the Eastern Glass Bottle Blowers' League, and the Western Green Bottle Blowers' Association, joined the Knights. The American Flint Glass Workers Union, on the other hand, refused to go along with the other glassworkers because of an earlier dispute with the Order. In New York City the Knights made a determined but unsuccessful attempt to capture the German shoemakers and the Associated Jewelers. Most of the larger and more important unions emphatically rejected the Order's overtures. The members of the Amalgamated Association of Iron and Steel Workers overwhelmingly defeated a referendum on the subject, while a similar poll conducted by the secretary of the Bricklayers and Masons resulted in the same conclusion. The Iron Molders' convention turned down the merger proposal by a vote of 114 to 27. Furthermore, the Typographical Union, the Carpenters, the Plumbers and Gas Fitters, the coal miners, and the Stationary Engineers all rejected the invitation to join the Knights.

At the regular meeting of the General Assembly in October 1886 further negotiations between the trade unions and the Knights again ended in failure. The action by the Assembly in ordering all workers holding cards in both the Knights and the Cigar Makers International Union to leave the latter under pain of expulsion was interpreted by both sides as constituting a final break and an open declaration of war. The trade union committee therefore issued a call on November 19, 1866, for all unions to send representatives to a convention in Columbus, Ohio, on December 8, to form an "American Federation or Alliance of all National and International Trade Unions." Out of this meeting came the A.F. of L. Completely dominated by the national unions, the December convention excluded assemblies of the Knights from membership, and then proceeded to establish the new organization on a firm foundation.

Thus by the end of 1886 the die had been cast, and the Knights and national unions prepared for war. Why had all negotiations failed? Undoubtedly the intractability of leaders on both sides contributed to the difficulties, but there were also those who had made sincere efforts to head off the impending conflict. The trade unions, furthermore, had encountered jurisdictional rivalries with the Knights, but this has been an endemic problem of the labor movement, and one which has not always had an unhappy ending.

The conflict between the Knights and the trade unions, then, had a much broader significance than the negotiations between them indicated, and represented the culmination of decades of historical development. The Knights, growing out of the humanitarian and reform crusades of ante-bellum America, emphasized the abolition of the wage system and the reorganization of society. To achieve this purpose it insisted on the prime importance of the mixed assembly, which would serve as the nucleus of an organization dedicated to reform. The trade unions, on the other hand, accepted their environment, and sought to take advantage of the relative scarcity of labor and the rising scale of production. Hence they emphasized the collective bargaining functions of labor organizations, thus tacitly accepting the workers' wage status.

Perhaps grounds for compromise did exist, but neither side was prone to make any concessions. The national unions, by insisting upon strict trade autonomy as a *sine qua non* of settlement, were in effect demanding that the Knights should virtually abandon any pretense at being a bona fide labor organization. It is true that the unions could have organized as national autonomous trade districts if the Knights had been ready to grant permission. The leaders of the Knights, however, were unwilling to permit their organization to be transformed into what the A.F. of L. ultimately became. Indeed, after 1886 many national trade districts left the Order because of their inability to function within the framework of that body.[2] The national unions, moreover, were not encouraged by the experiences of trade districts within the Knights before 1886. Finally, there was the simple element of power, and both the trade unions and the Knights, as established organizations, were adamant in their refusal to surrender any part of it.

Between reform and trade unionism, therefore, existed a gulf that the leaders of the 1880's were unable to bridge. By 1886 this chasm had widened to such a degree that co-operation between the two seemed virtually impossible and war seemed to be the only solution. Reform and trade unionism had at last come to a parting of the ways, and upon the outcome of the ensuing struggle hinged the destiny of the American labor movement.

---

[2] The shoemakers, miners, machinists, garmentworkers, carriage and wagon-workers, and potters all seceded from the Knights after 1886 because of their inability to function efficiently within the existing framework of the Order.

The Carpenters:
A Case in Point

ROBERT CHRISTIE

A number of scholars—Gerald Grob among them—have analyzed the clash between reformism and trade unionism from the top. But how did the conflict work itself out concretely for a given group of workers? Thanks to Robert Christie's fine study of the carpenters, we can move from the general to the specific. The protagonist is Peter J. McGuire, one of the great labor reformers of the era. On the other side is the union that McGuire founded and long dominated, the United Brotherhood of Carpenters and Joiners. The union, responsive to technological changes in the industry and the job needs of its members, moved irresistibly in the direction of pure-and-simple unionism. The touchstone here, as Christie saw it, was the emergence of the business agent. Committed as he was to reform objectives, McGuire resisted the administrative mechanisms and narrow policies that would enable the Carpenters' Brotherhood to operate effectively as a business union. In the decade-long struggle that ensued, it was a foregone conclusion that McGuire would ultimately meet defeat at the hands of the business agents. No book better illuminates the clash between old and new in the labor movement, nor more fully captures the essence of the emergent business unionism, than does *Empire in Wood*.

THERE APPEARED IN *The Carpenter* OF JULY 1914 A PICTURE OF the carpenters who had erected the L. C. Smith Building. They stood on the roof of the completed building, a score or so of walrus-mustachioed old-time carpenters, glowering at the camera. Almost without exception, they had on under their overalls stiff collars, ties, and tie pins.

From Robert Christie, *Empire in Wood: A History of the Carpenters' Union,* Ithaca, New York: The New York State School of Industrial and Labor Relations, 1956, pp. 17–18, 26–30, 61–74, 79–90. Reprinted by permission of the publisher. Footnotes have been omitted except where they amplify the text.

They all wore white shirts, suit coats, and bowlers, derbies, or slouch felt hats. Those without overalls had gold watch chains and fobs stretched across their abundant middles. Their day, perhaps, has passed. The attire certainly has. But it goes a long way toward symbolizing the old-time carpenter's craft pride and character: he came to work attired like his boss. He took pride in neither wearing gloves nor getting his hands very dirty. He worked with his hat on. At the day's end he took off his overalls, folded them atop his tools in the tool shed, washed his scarcely dirty hands, straightened his tie, tipped his bowler a bit more jauntily, and sought out the nearest bar.

Although the carpenter's craft pride and independence have changed but little since the first carpenter sawed the first piece of wood in America, his industry and his union have changed greatly since then. In fact, at one time, because industrial conditions made them unnecessary, the carpenters had no unions. It is in this period that a history of the United Brotherhood of Carpenters and Joiners of America properly begins.

☆   ☆   ☆

After 1871 a host of woodworking machine inventions rained down upon the unprotected craft. A sander which smoothed wood as fast as a dozen carpenters and a compound carver which turned out six wood duplicates and replaced three-score carpenters were but two of a series of such inventions which lured handicraft work into the factory and effected a major unheaval in the woodworking industry. Table I speaks for itself.

TABLE I   Hand and Machine Labor Costs in the Woodworking Industry: 1858 to 1896

Item	Years		Labor Cost	
	Hand	Machine	Hand	Machine
50 blinds..	1848	1896	$ 87	$ 8.00
12 mantel brackets............................	1889	1896	112	46.00
50 white pine doors...........................	1894	1895	113	11.00
1,000 ft. 4½″ yellow pine ceiling......	1859	1895	14	.44
1,000 ft. 3″ oak flooring...................	1858	1895	21	.54
1,000 ft. 4½″ yellow pine flooring....	1859	1895	12	.36
50 pair yellow pine sashes.................	1858	1895	60	9.00
10 sets stair risers and treads............	1858	1895	26	2.00

The first effect of machine inventions was to give birth to the "green hand"—a woman, an immigrant, or child—who displaced a score of carpenters at half the wages of one. One labor paper held in 1877 that "as improved . . . machinery has advanced . . . hundreds of thousands [of workers] have been . . . thrown in idleness on the pavement. In proof of this it is only necessary to refer to carpentry . . . thousands upon thousands of whose members have been reduced to want."

The windows, doors, and other parts of the building which streamed off the machine, standardized, complete, and ready for installation, allowed for the easy subdivision of the carpenter's work. Carpentry was gradually divided into door hanging, floor laying, stair building, and a score of other special tasks by competing contractors who only paid one-half the wage of a fully trained, all-around carpenter. By the early 1880's Peter J. Mc-Guire, the founder of the Carpenters' Union, complained that "in a few weeks . . . a lad becomes proficient in his part [of the carpenter's craft]." While this lad may have been a "proficient" window setter or shingle installer, he was not a carpenter. He was the outside green hand.

Harassed both in the factory and outside on the building site by the green hand, the carpenter rapidly discovered that still another evil stemmed from the advent of woodworking machinery: piecework. The steady stream of ready-to-install parts which poured off the machines were ideally suited to this mode of payment. And piecework, in turn, was ideally suited to the speed-up. One carpenter complained in 1876 that he had become a floor layer, that he received twenty-five cents for each "square" he laid, and that he was able to lay only three a day.

The pieceworking system effected a basic change in the organization of the industry. Prior to 1872, while the building might have been financed for resale by the speculator, the speculator dealt with one contractor who supplied both labor and material. After the advent of the pieceworker, however:

> Speculators . . . [started] putting up shoddy houses on ninety day builders' loans. . . . One of the curses in the carpentry work on these shoddy houses is the system of lumping and subletting or piecework. The lumper . . . takes a whole job at a certain figure; he then sublets it to another, who, in turn, parcels it out to others, who do the work in as rapid . . . a manner as possible—tearing and rushing to get it done. They all have to make a profit, at the expense of [both] the buyer and the laborer.

This "speculator" was the hated middleman, who by 1881 was encamped on the carpenter's very doorstep. Under the aegis of the piece-work-subcontracting system, he threatened to preside over the disintegration of the carpenter's craft. The most naïve carpenter could no longer question the middleman's identity. He had but to find any green hand butchering wood and there behind him, often literally driving him to greater production, stood the hated middleman. The new speculator and his half-carpenter green hand not only justified a half-century of abstract hatred for the middleman but also anchored it firmly in economic fact. The pieceworker allowed the carpenter to be both philosophical and practical, antimiddleman and job conscious, at the same time. Through the medium of the pieceworker, a half-century of vague antimiddleman sentiment was translated into specific and pragmatic trade union principles.

Consequently, the carpenters were finally able to formulate a logical and consistent trade union philosophy which took into account the working carpenter's grievances and promised to redress them through the medium of a national union. The Brotherhood of Carpenters and Joiners of America was a conscious outgrowth of this philosophy which, for the first twenty years of its existence, colored its every activity.

☆   ☆   ☆

The philosophy of the founders of the union began with a hatred of the pieceworker that was two parts scorn. He was held to be a poor befuddled fool, a "botch." The system, not the man, was at fault. If you wish to hate any class of men, hate the middleman, the monopolist, the speculator, the capitalist. For all these were one man and the pieceworker his pliant tool. The pieceworker was thus only a point of departure for a broad socialist philosophy. All this the founders told the carpenters.

This philosophy was propounded and applied by one man, Peter J. McGuire. For twenty years his personality and philosophy dominated the union. Almost singlehandedly he founded and raised the Brotherhood of Carpenters and Joiners of America to unchallenged pre-eminence among American unions.

McGuire was born of Irish immigrant parents in 1852 on New York's lower East Side. He received little formal schooling before being apprenticed as a joiner in 1867. At night, however, he attended the free lectures and courses at the Cooper Union, then a gathering place for the city's radical and discontented. There he acquired a life-long interest in what scholars then called political economy. Once launched on a study of society, it took him little time to become an advocate of its most violent reorganization. Before he was twenty, he was described by Gompers as an intelligent, big-hearted, but violent and radical advocate of the working-class cause.

☆   ☆   ☆

McGuire purposely created a weak national administration which reflected his broad educational ends and his organize-agitate-educate means.

While his matchless, almost evangelical, skill as an organizer lured thousands of new carpenters into local unions, it did not guarantee their staying there. As a result, during the 1880's and early 1890's local unionists devised for themselves trade union institutions designed to fill the carpenters' day-to-day needs. If these institutions developed along lines hardly foreseen by McGuire, they sprang, at least at the outset, from McGuire's philosophy.

McGuire did not want to destroy capitalism but to have it taken over by the trade unions. He harbored no animus against capitalists as organizers of productive labor. Rather, he made a fine and perhaps untenable distinction between a capitalist as an organizer of labor and a nonproducing and speculative middleman. As a result, the first Brotherhood carpenters bore little malice toward their immediate employers if they were "genuine" contractors; that is, if they provided materials as well as labor and did not work by the subcontract, hire piece-or-lump workers, or allow work done for them to be lumped. The leaders of the early Brotherhood believed that the legitimate contractor had as much to lose to the pieceworker as did the carpenter. One of the first editions of *The Carpenter* held that "with the workmen . . . thoroughly organized . . . we can soon arrive at a harmonious understanding [to end piecework] with the better class of contractors and boss builders."

Early Brotherhood leaders encouraged the various locals to bargain, conciliate, and even arbitrate, rather than strike the better class of regular contractors. In the spring of 1882 Gabriel Edmonston, through his local, Number One of Washington, D.C., encouraged the bosses to form an employers' organization. In May its formation was announced. Local Union One agreed that its journeymen were to work for none but "genuine" contractors, and the employers agreed to employ only "genuine" carpenters. In New York and Brooklyn, mass meetings were held in 1882 in conjunction with "genuine" contractors. Together, the unionists and their bosses pledged that they would take joint steps to eliminate piecework, which led to intense competition injurious to both contractor and carpenter. Thus the piece-rate system channeled the carpenter's disaffection away from his immediate employer and toward the middleman and established the climate of feeling out of which collective bargaining was later to grow.

High-sounding joint declarations, however, did but little to stop the pieceworker, who was difficult to find, much less eradicate. Working as a subcontractor, he took flash jobs which often were completed in as little as a few days, a week at the most. He moved into a half-completed row of homes or apartments, received material from the speculator, installed the doors, stairs, or windows, packed his tools, and stole silently away.

The "genuine" contractors were powerless to combat the pieceworker. Only the union, through the medium of a paid and full-time representative with power to strike immediately any job on which piecework appeared, could combat him. Thus was born the office of business agent.

Carpenter James Lynch, who was probably the first business agent, described in his own words how the post was created.

A large number of brown-stone fronts were being built by speculators [in New York City]. They would build a block seven hundred feet long and four or five stories high; letting out such work as setting door frames to one class of men at so much each; the putting on of casings to another. This led to special classes of workers known as "doorhangers," etc., according to their special work.

While this practice was strenuously opposed by the union, still it was unable to stop it, as these men were outside of the union and worked all sorts of hours.

In desperation, it was decided to pay a representative to keep after them, so in July, 1883, a walking delegate of the Carpenters of New York City was appointed.

Thus I was taken from the executive office of the Carpenters of New York City and became their *first walking delegate*.

At first the functions of the business agent were not clearly defined and he was called "walking delegate" or "special agent." In some cases he was part of a "committee of walking delegates." As his functions became clearly defined, however, he came to be known as a business agent. By 1890 McGuire reported that a full one hundred cities had business agents. In the following years the business agent was recognized for the first time as an official person by the executive board when it decided that the business agent could be empowered to "collect dues and et cetera." In 1892 McGuide remarked that the use of business agents had become the general custom.

A full-time, paid agent was an expense which few locals could or would carry alone. Hence the district council of local unions also came into being with the business agent. This organization is what the name implies, a council of the representatives of local unions of a given city or other closely knit area, empowered to conduct that portion of local affairs which can best be handled by a body with broader jurisdiction. Quite often the first proud notice that a city, Boston for instance, now had a full-time business agent was accomplished by the announcement that the Boston locals had banded together to pay for this luxury.

McGuire announced in 1888 that, while district councils were not yet mandatory, they had sprung up in at least fourteen cities. Following his advice, the 1888 convention made it mandatory for the carpenters of any city with two or more local unions to form a district council. In 1890 there were twenty-six district councils, and they were given power to regulate all strikes. Two years later McGuire reported thirty-two district councils, and they were given all disciplinary power which had previously belonged to the locals. These moves amounted to a mass transfer of administrative, and hence of political, power from the local union to the district council. After 1892 the district council was the real, basic administrative unit of the Brotherhood.

Operating through the district council, the business agent came to fulfill many tasks (other than controlling the pieceworker) which before his advent had gone begging. He effectively negotiated with employers who had previously blackballed any working carpenter presenting union demands. In cooperation with business agents of other crafts, he helped to coordinate and to administer all building trades strike efforts. With his knowledge of the supply of and demand for carpenters, he was able to help the locals regulate the labor market. He became, in effect, a one-man employment bureau with complete knowledge of all new jobs in this casual industry. By maintaining craft standards and eliminating the pieceworker, he aided management as well as the carpenters. He was, in short, a small labor contractor who served employer and employee alike, a middleman. This is a fact of basic importance to both the past and future development of the United Brotherhood. To establish its full significance, it is necessary to retrace several developments up to 1890.

It will be recalled that the first carpenters' unions arose out of protest against the middleman, and that during the nineteenth century, the carpenter joined with the rest of the labor and reform movement in fostering an antimiddleman or producer-conscious type of trade unionism. The Brotherhood was founded in this tradition, and its first leaders hoped, through the medium of trade unions, to eliminate the middleman as an economic being and then to inaugurate a producers' commonwealth. The carpenter's strong desire to become his own boss, however, struggled with his hatred for the middleman, and he aided and abetted the middleman by taking up piecework. In the eight-hour movement the carpenter, who had previously refused to trade piecework for the vague hope of a producers' commonwealth, traded it for the tangible and immediate gain of shorter hours.

By 1890 it was evident that the system of speculation and subcontracting which has since characterized the industry was there to stay. The carpenters were not as anxious to overthrow this system as they were to control it. Unable to defeat the system, they became a part of it. In order to represent the carpenters' interests, the business agents became middlemen who contracted for labor. Thus did "business" unionism, for the carpenter's craft, at least, have its genesis.

The sum of the business agent's activities clearly established him as a labor contractor. He promised to deliver to the employer a certain number of carpenters possessed of a certain guaranteed degree of skill at a stated time for a stated wage. With the employers or their agents he annually signed a written contract clearly stipulating these promises. In return he received the right to control fully the trade in a given community, to bargain for the wages and working conditions received by the men he supplied, and to replace the old speculator contractor and his pieceworking carpenters as a labor-contractor-middleman.

Here, in the business agent's role as middleman, is the key to the conservatism of the Brotherhood and of building trades unions in general. The building trades business agent is a more vital part of his industry than are local union officers in any other industry. The industry is literally organized about his figure and functions. Because of his essential role, building trades unions were among the first and most successful in the American labor movement. By the same token, the building trades unions are among the most conservative. For the business agent is not alone an organizer of workers' discontent. He is also a middleman around whom the building industry is constructed. What his left or union hand may choose to do may grievously harm his right or middleman's hand. Thus while the business agent enjoys a position of strength which makes him the envy of many another local union officer, he also bears a burden of industrial responsibility which at times becomes crushing. McGuire's abstract radicalism was a luxury he perhaps could afford. With his strange dual function it was a luxury hardly available to the business agent.

Such a man was not only a middleman, he was also a career man in the trade union field, a professional organizer, a union executive, a member of a union bureaucracy. The union provided his opportunity to rise in the world, to associate with and to ape his boss, and perhaps to climb a bit higher than he. When he obtained his goals, the institutions which had borne him upward became vested interests to be changed as infrequently as possible. He had a stake in the union, the industry, and the community. He decried and deplored every radical manifestation. He was completely dedicated to the present order as long as it provided a niche for his brand of trade unionism.

A glance at the career of any one of these new local leaders bears out their nature as professional bureaucrats. Frank Duffy was the salaried national secretary of the United Brotherhood for over forty years. Before assuming that position in 1901, he held the following offices: representative of Local Union 478 to the New York District Council, thirteen successive times; financial secretary of Local Union 478, four times; business agent, 1896 to 1898; president of the executive council of the New York District Council, six successive times; delegate to the United Brotherhood conventions of 1896, 1898, and 1900; and executive board member, 1900 to 1901. Duffy's career is typical of that of a whole host of young men who rose to power on the local level during the 1890's.

No group could have contrasted more sharply with McGuire than did these men, his followers. They looked different. McGuire was unkempt, with a long drooping mustache and deep-set, burning eyes. He was given to riding freights and to fiery radical oratory, while Harry Lloyd, leader of the Boston District Council, was described as "a good speaker and fair and conservative in all he had to say. He dressed well in dark clothes, wore a heavy gold chain and charm and might have been mistaken for a young lawyer."

They spoke different words. In 1891 McGuire gave his opinion about the ultimate goals of trade unions:

> To educate our class, to prepare it for the changes to come, to establish a system of co-operative industry in place of the wage system, to emancipate the workers from subjugation to the capitalists, these are our ultimate objects.

* * *

> We are approaching a great revolution, which if based upon organized action, is destined to assume control of the industries and the government of the nation.

A few years later William Huber, a Yonkers, New York, leader, might have been talking about McGuire when he criticized Socialists for being

> ... visionary, their schemes and isms are only the mouthings of a lot of irresponsible, imaginative fantastical doctrinaires. . . . Our local unions are . . . being contaminated by even permitting one of their disciples to pollute the floor of their hall and the air of their meeting room with his foul harrange of sedition . . . I . . . have taken steps to cleanse the labor firmament of their scurrilous and untruthful literature and proselytizing emissaries.

As the conservative career trade unionists came to fill out the complement of local leadership after 1890, McGuire became strangely out of place in his own union. With his violent desire to reorganize society, he was as incompatible with these men as a Communist would have been at a 1950 college fraternity convention. For in 1890, as he had been in 1881 and as he was to be till the day he died, McGuire was an extreme, intelligent, undisciplined, selfless, disorganized radical of the old American school who could have walked lightly beside Tom Paine or Sam Adams. When he stood on a platform beside the professional organizers, nine-teenth- and twentieth-century trade unionism met. Like oil and water, they did not mingle.

Rather, they drew apart, for McGuire would not create, nor allow others to create, an administrative nexus between the national office and the local bodies. In spite of the phenomenal success of his organizing activity, for the first nine years of its existence the union had no national administration worthy of the name. Many experiments were tried. None of them changed the essential fact that the United Brotherhood in 1890 was still being ruled along lines set down for the little reform organization founded by a group of mad-at-the-world, down-at-the-heel reformers a decade earlier.

McGuire consciously blocked the growth of an administrative hierarchy which would have linked the district councils closely with the national office. In 1884 he suggested that perhaps too many dollars were being sent to the national office by the locals. His methods, he said, were simple and required only enough dollars to carry on the educational campaign. In 1891 he said:

> The tendency of the labor movement is towards simplicity, autonomy and federation. Simplicity of organization, autonomy of function and federation of interests. Workmen have no use for complicated machinery with intricate cogs and wheels in labor organizations. The simpler it is the better [it is] understood.

These words welled out of a strongly held and carefully thought-out conviction about the function and goals of the trade union. McGuire wanted simplicity of organization because he felt that the workers would not become truly active in a union with machinery too complex for them to understand. At best, such a union would attract a group of dues-paying automatons who would allow self-interested trade union politicians to rule for them. When union politicians enter, Socialists exit; they are forced out or they cease being Socialists. And McGuire, as will become clear later, remained a Socialist until he died.

He dreaded, as did so many old Socialists, that trade unionism would become an end in itself; that it would be absorbed by and become an adjunct to capitalism if its machinery became too complex, if it became an accepted institution. He saw trade unions as a funnel through which workers were passed on their journey to socialism. The trade union's main function was to educate, and no elaborate administrative machinery was needed for this task, only "agitators."

As a result, in 1890 the national office had no regional representatives of any kind, no paid and full-time president or executive board, no organizers. There existed no lines of communication between McGuire and the various district councils except that which McGuire provided personally. There did, however, exist strong reasons for erecting such lines. There were the professional organizers. These composed a group of young, ambitious men whose activities were confined to the district council level as long as McGuire would not create regional organizations and expand the national office. They could not become regional vice-presidents or full-time members of the executive board because such posts did not exist. Nor could they become organizers for the same reason. Their ambitions, held unnaturally in check, represented an ominous force which under pressure might burst the bounds of McGuire's paternalistic rule.

And in 1890 the pressure for an expanded national administration was mounting for several reasons. First, the United Order carpenters were trade union members of twenty years' standing in 1890. They had not been organized by McGuire, the United Brotherhood, or its eight-hour movement. They owed little to the national office and could hardly be expected to tolerate long an executive board elected, as it had been since 1884, by the carpenters of one city, Philadelphia. Beside this unrest can be placed the continued technological development of the woodworking industry as a source of pressure for an expanded national office. Woodworking mills were taking an increasingly greater toll of carpenters' work. Mill owners were moving to the countryside to avoid the new and more efficient district council organization of the Brotherhood which was evolving between 1886 and 1890. There advantage could be taken of child, female, and immigrant labor, without fear of interference from the district councils.

The district councils attempted to cope with the threat posed by "unfair, country building material" by binding their employers to use only "union, *city-made* materials." Since country mills lay beyond the jurisdiction of any city district council, however, and since one country mill might market its products in several different district council jurisdictions, only an organizational drive with intercity direction could effectively cope with them. An executive board composed of members from one city was incapable of such direction.

The employers provided a third source of pressure for an expanded national office. After the initial successes of the 1886 eight-hour movement, the builders took a lesson from the union book and in 1887 banded together as the National Builders' Association. They were led by George Prussing of Chicago, Marc Eidlitz of New York, and E. E. Scribner of St. Louis. The new organization threw all of its weight behind counteroffensives in the spring of 1887. In Chicago it fought the Carpenters to a draw, and in Toronto defeated them with lockouts.

By the time of the 1890 eight-hour strikes, the builders had tightened their organization and introduced a new arsenal of weapons in their war against the Carpenters. They first used the secondary boycott in the building industry, applying pressure on building material firms to refuse materials to union contractors. The National Builders' Association assisted its affiliated organizations just as the United Brotherhood did its locals by extending them financial aid to resist strikes. This organized opposition took the edge off many of the larger 1890 strikes, and in Wheeling, West Virginia, and Portland, Oregon, two of the larger strikes were defeated outright. In the following spring two huge strikes in Newark, New Jersey, and Pittsburgh, Pennsylvania, into which the national office had poured over $19,000, were defeated by organized employers' resistance. Important strikes were also lost in 1891 in San Francisco, New Orleans, Chattanooga, Seattle, and six other cities across the nation.

It was out of one such Chicago strike that the first mild attack upon McGuire stemmed. The strikers were receiving financial aid from the national office when in May, 1890, they asked for the assistance of a national officer. The Philadelphia executive board dispatched part-time President Rowland to Chicago. Rowland found that the National Builders' Association was systematically importing strikebreakers, financing resistance to the strike, and bringing the carpenter leaders into court constantly on conspiracy and picketing charges.

However, Rowland also found that the Chicago leaders had organized the strike well and that the carpenters were standing firm behind them. Unionists picketed railroad stations for a sixty-five mile radius about Chicago, warning itinerant carpenters of the strike. The Chicago leaders had also initiated a countersuit against the employers for violation of the alien contract labor law by their importation of Canadian carpenters.

Public pressure, however, was mounting against the strikers. Under this pressure, without any consideration of the tactical situation in Chicago, the Philadelphia executive board wired Rowland on April 24 to accept any terms the contractors offered. Rowland felt that such a step would be disastrous in light of local conditions. It would be interpreted as a sellout by the Chicago carpenters and might lose the Brotherhood its Chicago membership. He defied the board members on the ground that he was more conversant with the Chicago situation than they. His decision held, despite the executive board's charge of insubordination, and the strike was later settled by arbitration. Strong employers' resistance met at other points in the eight-hour drive of 1890 demonstrated the inability of a one-city executive board to cope with a national employers' association, and financial aid was withdrawn from strikes in Boston, Philadelphia, Detroit, Louisville, and Portland, in June, 1890.

Pressure for a revised national administration was strong and mounting when the 1890 convention opened. There could have been little doubt in McGuire's mind about the reforms desired by the professional organizers. They wished to have full-time and regionally elected executive board members with power to employ organizers. In 1887 the Massachusetts locals had sent on their own initiative a referendum vote on this question, but McGuire had declared it illegal. Later in that same year the Massachusetts locals tried to form a state organization which McGuire also quashed. At the 1888 convention the local leaders actually succeeded in creating a Board of Seven Vice Presidents, regionally elected, to help the Philadelphia executive board run the organization. However, this board only met once a year, had no control over finances, and served only to harass the Philadelphia executive board. From 1888 to 1890 the two boards' incessant clashing made a farce of the national administration. At first, McGuire, quite satisfied with the easy-to-handle Philadelphia executive board, stood aloof. Then, having gauged the extent of the professional organizers' strength, he moved to still their protest. At the 1890 convention he shifted his support from the Philadelphia executive board to the new board of vice-presidents and presented the delegates with a new constitution drawn up by himself for their approval.

The new constitution met only one of the demands of the professional organizers and that only part of the way. It created a five-man executive board composed of representatives from each of five districts into which the nation was divided. Its members, however, were not paid and met only four times a year. Further, they were not elected exclusively by members of their districts but by the convention at large. They were given no power to appoint full-time and paid organizers. While a step away from the old one-city executive board, the step was but a short one. The other provisions of the constitution were many, but they changed little that was basic. Administered in McGuire's slipshod fashion, they left the national organization much the same in 1891 as it had been in 1889: a one-man show.

Clinging doggedly to his socialistic aims and educational tactics, McGuire absorbed more and more of the functions of the national office until the man and the office were indistinguishable. The building in which the United Brotherhood had offices, the records, office supplies, and even the general fund of the union were owned in his name. As one of his contemporaries, Frank Duffy, said, "McGuire could have said to the Executive Board, 'Here, gentlemen, get out of this building [the Brotherhood's headquarters], this place belongs to me.'" John Williams, the eleventh general president, summed up the nature of McGuire's rule when he said:

> It [the union] was dominated in every vital respect by one forceful personality. All administrative functions were centered in one official.

• • •

> The serious minded and earnest men who in various sections of the country were leading the Brotherhood [during the 1890's] knew that growth such as they had a right to look for was out of the question until the organization was unshackled and freed from the bonds of a form of paternalism that repressed its spirit and stunted its growth. I know that this was their feeling but they withheld expression thereof because of their loyalty and affection for a great leader and a masterful mind.

Thus in 1892 the Brotherhood faced a strange dilemma. On one hand stood a group of professional trade union career men strongly entrenched behind local institutions of their own creation. On the other stood one of the most fabled figures of nineteenth-century radicalism, as strongly entrenched behind a name and a reputation. While he had built no institutions, he had created the union, through which the local leaders had risen to power. The local leaders were too strongly entrenched behind the real economic power of their business agents to be overthrown on their home grounds. And the personal loyalty which McGuire inspired in the rank and file was too strong for the new leaders to budge him. Either the professional organizers or the philosopher organizer had to give ground if the union was to prosper. Neither gave ground. In 1892 McGuire entered into a ten-year fight with the professional organizers.

☆   ☆   ☆

In their two direct and crude attempts to depose McGuire, the new leaders had learned a painful lesson: not so easily is a king dethroned. Consequently they turned to a skillfully conceived method of wearing away the base of McGuire's power. In the execution of their plan, the new leaders received help from an unexpected quarter: an industrial revolution in the building industry. It had gained momentum in the late 1880's, and during the late 1890's, it broke over the heads of the building trades unionists with a force and fury sufficient to change the whole structure of the industry.

Prior to 1885 new methods of casting iron for lintels, beams, and girders enabled contractors to build to a height of five stories. The Chicago fire of 1871, however, proved the inadequacy of these structures when faced with the menace of fire. Before the skyscrapers could become an important factor in the American building industry, fireproofing was essential. When in 1885 commercial production of rolled or structural steel was rendered possible under the Bessemer process, the industrial revolution got under way. Steel made in this manner, when properly protected, was fireproof. By 1900 structural steel had replaced cast iron in most modern construction.

Before buildings could soar to new heights, however, the elevator was necessary. W. B. Baxter, Jr., developed an electrically powered elevator in Baltimore in 1887. Two years later N. P. Otis developed a more successful one in New York City. After Otis founded his company in 1904, the elevator became standard in large buildings, both during and after construction. The elevator combined with new riveting processes to make possible the steel skeleton around which modern skyscrapers are built. The Waldorf Astoria Hotel in New York City was the first building to use both of these new developments in its construction in 1890.

The huge weight of the skyscraper called forth new engineering developments in the field of foundations. After years of experimenting, construction engineers used caissons and compressed air to create bedrock foundations for the Manhattan Life Insurance Company Building and the Mutual Life Insurance Company Building, erected in New York City between 1893 and 1900.

Fifteen years before 1900, E. L. Ransome of San Francisco had invented the twisted bar of steel and had demonstrated that it could be encased in cement to produce reinforced concrete. Gradually during the 1890's this new material replaced the older brick and masonry as filling for the steel skeleton of buildings. By 1905 reinforced concrete had passed the experimental stage.

These and other inventions and processes completely changed the structure of the building industry by the turn of the century. Twenty-five years later, George Otis Smith, director of the United States Geological Survey, could say that to erect a modern building one had but to

> take by weight sixty parts of gravel, sand, and crushed stone; fifty-eight parts of tile and brick; twenty-seven parts of building stone; nineteen parts of cement and sixteen parts of steel, with such other ingredients as copper and glass and asbestos and paint . . . to suit one's taste.

This revolution in building techniques affected the carpenter in four specific ways. First, it changed his most important source of employment from small, local contractors to large, intercity construction firms. The small contractor, even when backed by a wealthy speculator, could not undertake the building of a huge skyscraper. The cost of the new equipment alone demanded huge construction companies which had to be highly mobile if they were to keep their expensive capital equipment occupied. Hence large intercity construction companies burgeoned in the 1890's. In 1911 Gompers estimated that "probably a dozen or more great building contractors . . . do nearly all the construction of modern business buildings throughout the continent of America."

Its second effect was to create an even greater demand for the specialist carpenter. The modern skyscraper had ten, fourteen, even twenty stories of standardized rooms, each with the same floor, door, window, and wall measurements. It became an even simpler task for the contractor to hire a carpenter skilled in only one phase of his task. Consequently a whole spate of specialist carpenters' unions cropped up. By 1904 the general secretary reported the formation of unions among locomotive woodworkers, millwrights, shinglers, dock, wharf, and bridge builders, ceiling woodworkers, and carpenters' helpers.

Third, it created new crafts such as the sheet-metal workers, plumbers, and electricians, many of whom worked on material which replaced wood, and all of whom, while jurisdictional lines were fluid, usurped woodwork related to their job. Complaint against "other trades encroaching upon and stealing our work" was registered at the 1898 convention. By 1904 the delegate from Boston Local 33 complained that "the trade . . . is being taken, piece by piece, from our control . . . [by] the Electrical Workers, Wood, Wire and Metal Lathers, Building Laborers, and Sheet Metal Workers."

Fourth, the revolution in building techniques intensified the effect of woodworking mills upon the outside carpenter. The floors upon floors of standardized fixtures in a large skyscraper were easily produced by machine. More and more of the carpenter's work disappeared into planing mills. To add further to the carpenter's troubles, a new union, the Machine Wood Workers' International Union, stepped into the picture to claim jurisdiction over these "machine carpenters."

Each problem raised by the revolution in building techniques was a national one. The new construction companies were nation-wide in scope. The small specialist carpenters' unions drew members from all parts of the country. The new trades subsisting partly on work traditionally belonging to the carpenter had a national jurisdiction, as did the new union in the woodworking industry. National problems demanded solutions on a national scale. In addition, the last three of these four problems were jurisdictional in nature. The specialist carpenters' unions, the new trades, and the new woodworkers' unions all fattened themselves on portions of the carpenter's jurisdiction. The United Brotherhood, more than ever, had to devise jurisdictional policies on the national level which could be put into effect simultaneously in every district council in the land. This, in turn, called for a union with a strong, centralized administration and centrally directed agents, in all localities, ready to move at a moment's notice. In sum, the revolution in building techniques gave further economic and institutional substance to the administrative reforms for which the professional organizers had long been clamoring.

The jurisdictional problem served to initiate the last and most stormy of the struggles over administration which took place during the McGuire period. On the subject of jurisdictional expansion, McGuire was clearly a "little Englander." In 1900 he told President Huber that the Brotherhood, with eight hundred locals, was becoming too large for its own good and was getting "top heavy." Earlier, in 1894, he lamented the loss of half of the membership but saw it as a good omen inasmuch as the organization was shaking itself down to a hard core of good union men. "We have grown," he said in 1902, "but we have grown at an accelerated pace, a pace that is dangerous and we must . . . take means and care to preserve this organization."

McGuire was well aware that for every new member the Machine Woodworkers' Union gained, the Brotherhood would sooner or later lose one. He, however, did not care for the race to obtain dues payers. The important thing was to *unionize* the workers. It did not matter to him whether the worker entered the labor movement through this or that union. The important thing was that he enter the *movement*. McGuire was emotionally obsessed with a concept of united labor and not with the concerns of any given union. "Even though McGuire was the mainstay of his struggling organization, he found time for the . . . work of the Federation," said Gompers.

True, McGuire had fought the Knights of Labor and the United Order, but he fought them reluctantly and because of structural differences. He felt that each of the two unions was, in its own way, staying the unity of labor. Once unity was achieved through the AFL, however, McGuire saw no further reason for unions to quarrel over membership. It is doubtful if he would have mourned greatly had technological evolution wiped out the Brotherhood, providing that its members were absorbed by other AFL unions.

After 1885 McGuire allowed the leaders of the AFL to organize machine woodworkers. In 1888 he actually asked the carpenters to assist the International Furniture Workers' Union with the formation of locals of factory woodworkers. Finally, the United Brotherhood gave Gompers permission to charter the new International Union of Machine Wood Workers as a full-fledged AFL affiliate. Even Edmonston, who usually sided with Mc-

Guire, said of this move, "I can account for this . . . only by supposing . . . [McGuire] was hypnotized by the diplomacy of [Secretary] Thomas Kidd of the Woodworkers."

Trouble immediately arose on the local level between the United Brotherhood's professional organizers and the Wood Workers. In New York City, which used more wood trim than any other city and manufactured more than most other cities, the dispute crystallized earliest. Armed with his new AFL charter, Kidd sent organizer Richard Braunschweig to New York City just as United Brotherhood Local 309 was to set to sign a contract with Brunswick, Balke, Collender, and Company, one of the largest building fixture manufacturers. Braunschweig intruded with an offer to supply labor for seven cents an hour less than the Brotherhood offered. The firm signed with him, and he recruited nonunion labor through an "employment office" in the Bowery. These "carpenters" he then organized as Local Union 172 of the Machine Wood Workers' Union. He had neatly edged Local Union 309 out of the picture.

A violent dispute between the two unions ensued. To discover who first scabbed on whom is impossible. The dispute hung fire through executive board meetings and conventions of both unions until 1894. Kidd appeared before the 1894 convention of the Carpenters and asked that they give all of the machine woodworkers to his union. The delegates complied with his request because, Kidd felt, lacking a label and a system of organizers they were unable to unionize the mills. Jurisdiction over all woodworkers was given to the Machine Wood Workers' Union and all United Brotherhood locals were ordered to help the Machine Wood Workers to organize in the future. McGuire's successors were to rue the day pen ever met paper to consummate this, the "Indianapolis Agreement."

The Machine Wood Workers' Union and the other union then active in the woodworking industry, the International Furniture Workers' Union, decided to take advantage of the United Brotherhood's friendliness to broach the subject of amalgamation. The Furniture Workers and the Wood Workers had had jurisdictional disputes with each other as well as with the Carpenters. Both possessed, as well, a strong group of old-fashioned German Socialists who were inclined toward industrial unionism and who thought amalgamation a good first step.

In January, 1895, the executive board of the United Brotherhood approved a three-sided amalgamation conference. But McGuire, in keeping with his "little England" policy, flatly rejected the amalgamation offer extended at the conference. The Machine Wood Workers and the Furniture Workers then amalgamated without the Carpenters and formed the Amalgamated Wood Workers' International Union in late 1895.

In spite of the amalgamation, McGuire stood by the Indianapolis agreement. But this was the period (1894 to 1896) during which he was gradually losing his once viselike grip on the organization. To make a national agreement was no guarantee of its fulfillment on the local level. Several of the United Brotherhood locals objectted to the agreement and took in renegade Furniture Workers locals which had objected to the amalgamation.

While all this happened, the mill owners took advantage of the lull in union watchfulness to increase their rate of migration from New York and other urban centers into the hinterlands. One of the principal contractors in New York City described the exodus:

> Ten years ago . . . [in 1890] the great majority of doors, sashes, blinds, and trim . . . were manufactured within the limits of what today is known as Greater New York. Today . . . not twenty percent of it is manufactured there, and the other eighty percent is shipped, some as far as from Detroit and even west of there.

When "suburban" mills started flooding the New York market with cheap trim, the New York District Council began to complain. Later, the New York carpenters decided to refuse to handle "unfair, out-of-town" trim. In 1896 an "agitation against cheap, unfair, nonunion trim made in outside towns" was started. It enjoyed some measure of success in Stamford, Connecticut, and in Batavia and Rochester, New York.

When the 1896 convention of the Brotherhood met, feelings ran high on the related subjects of unfair trim and the Amalgamated Wood Workers' Union. They were contributing factors to the 1896 revolution against McGuire already described. McGuire had not only done little to help organize the country mills, but he had also seemingly sided with the Amalgamated Wood Workers. Though pressed to repudiate the Indianapolis agreement, he refused. Such a repudiation would have violated his sense of labor unity and would have added to what he felt was the all-too-rapid growth of the union.

Just as he had sloughed off the attack against his personal powers in 1896, so did he slough off this assault against his jurisdictional policy. The rebels were told that the United Brotherhood would continue to make agreements with other organizations when such agreements tended to promote harmony.

As the struggle against the Amalgamated Wood Workers' Union spread, the clamor against the Indianapolis agreement mounted. In July 1897 the executive board repudiated it, claiming somewhat belatedly that the amalgamation which created the Wood Workers' Union had rendered it void. The board requested that the Wood Workers' Union surrender to the United Brotherhood all mill work which was erected by the carpenter.

In a later conference with representatives of the Amalgamated Wood Workers, however, McGuire ignored the board and allowed the Wood Workers to retain jurisdiction over all planing mills, with the exception of those already organized by the United Brotherhood.

The New York District Council immediately protested this agreement, but McGuire replied that the executive board possessed the power to effect such a treaty and that their complaint was poorly taken. Again, in May, the New York District Council protested that Amalgamated Wood Worker members in Newark accepted a lower wage rate than did United Brotherhood mill-workers, As a result, mills organized by the United Brotherhood could not compete with those organized by the Amalgamated Wood Workers in the open market. The New York District Council leaders asked permission to take in Amalgamated Wood Workers. The executive board replied that the agreement stood, but Kidd would be asked to raise his men's wages in and about New York City.

McGuire courted disaster when he hit the independent, willful, conservative New York unions in their pocketbooks. His jurisdictional policy united the various groups displeased with his rule. Since the fiascos of 1894 and 1896 had taught the opposition the folly of a direct personal assault on McGuire, they turned to a plot which was later described by Executive Board Member John W. Williams:

The Committee on [the] Constitution of the 1898 Convention, with A. C. Cattermull . . . as chairman and . . . [myself] as Secretary, undertook its task with seriousness of purpose and a definite appreciation of the primary needs of the Brotherhood. The Committee knew that the time had come to break away from the old order. . . . It knew that if the United Brotherhood was to fulfill its mission and to realize its possibilities, a new course had to be mapped out.

The first and most important step was the conversion of the office of the General President from a mere figurehead into an active and essential factor in the administration . . . of the organization. The Committee knew the fate of every previous effort to change the Constitution in regard to that office; therefore, it concluded not to recommend another attempt. Instead, it drew upon its practical knowledge of psychology for a plan to gain the result. It was agreed to put forth a number of changes in the Constitution whereby many and varied duties devolving upon the General Secretary were to be transferred to the General President. It was thought that the membership . . . would not oppose the idea of making the General President the actual, as well as the nominal, head of the organization, so long as it was done without providing . . . for another salaried office. The Committee also requested and received authority to prepare [instead of allowing, as had been the custom, McGuire to prepare for it] the official circular submitting the amendments . . . to a referendum. By this means any scheme that [McGuire] might have contemplated to defeat the plan was frustrated. How well the Committee on [the] Constitution and the Convention gauged the feeling and temper of the members is shown by the fact that out of about fifty . . . amendments . . . only two were defeated. Of the wisdom of the course adopted at that time there can be no shadow of a doubt.

In keeping with this strategy, the general president was given the duty of examining and approving all local constitutions and of deciding all grievances. In order better to explain the logic of his decisions to the members of the executive board, the general president was given voice but no vote on the board. Since none of these moves took any money from the close-fisted membership or substantially encroached on McGuire's province, the membership allowed them to stand. The conspirators hoped that when the newly empowered general president demonstrated his value to the organization, he would be given a salary. Until that time he was to make his way as best he could by working for the union at night. The first light taps of a divisive wedge had been struck.

On the subject of jurisdiction, the opposition moved forthrightly behind the leadership of the New York locals. Local Union 476 appealed to the convention against McGuire's 1897 treaty with the Amalgamated Wood Workers' Union. McGuire's convention committee upheld the treaty, but after an angry floor debate the delegates threw the torn-up treaty into his teeth by a decisive sixty-nine to forty vote. Then they revised the jurisdictional clause of the constitution so as to make it amply clear to all machine woodworkers that the Brotherhood was their home base. They also resolved that

. . . no other carpenters' or woodworkers' organizations of any kind be reeognized by the Brotherhood and that no agreement be entered into with other carpenters', woodworkers' or machine-hands' organizations by our general officers and further, that all agreements now existing be annulled.

McGuire's policy, if not McGuire, had been repudiated. Cattermull continued to head the executive board, and no less a person than J. W. Williams was elected general president.

With McGuire's peace-and-goodwill policy a shambles, events started to move rapidly. The New York unions held a monster rally to protest unfair trim, to serve notice on the Amalgamated Wood Workers, and to devise campaign strategy. At each of the 1899 meetings of the executive board the problem of organization was discussed. In January the board members decided that "something had to be done to strengthen and build up our organization" and ordered McGuire to prepare an organizing scheme. McGuire refused to suggest a plan, however, and at the April meeting handed the hot potato back to the board members. The board replied by arbitrarily appropriating $5,000 to finance four paid and full-time organizers. Three of the four, A. C. Cattermull, W. J. Shields, and W. J. Williams, were members of the executive board. Bit by bit, the organization was slipping through McGuire's hands, like rope in some gigantic tug of war in which the future was pitted against the past.

McGuire's tired body then came to the aid of the opposition by collapsing. In late 1899 and 1900 there were several notices of his sickness in *The Carpenter,* and just before the 1900 convention the members were advised that his health had failed because of "insomnia and nervous troubles." At this convention it seemed a simple matter to the opposition to consign McGuire and all his pathetic visions of utopia to limbo.

The opposition at the 1900 convention was led by William Huber, who had become general president when Williams resigned in 1899 to take a political appointment with the New York State government. A career trade union official of a decade's standing, he was a big, handsome, confident man, the complete apostle of the new, practical unionism. His presidential address to the 1900 convention brimmed with determination and firmness. This man would be no figurehead.

Huber led another frontal attack on the sick McGuire's powers. This time the assault centered about a specific and democratic plan to base the powers of the general officers upon the local membership. Each state was to be designated a "section." Each section was to have a convention in advance of the general convention and was to send instruction-bound delegates, at the rate of one per thousand members, to the general convention. Mileage to and from the national convention was to be paid all delegates by the national office.

The plan was an obvious advance. It based the convention on real units of local power and eliminated rotten borough locals as convention representation units. By paying their fares, it encouraged each section to send its delegates. By binding the delegates with instructions, it prevented administration control of the convention through logrolling deals. Frank Duffy, who was later to become McGuire's successor and Huber's aide-de-camp, headed the committee which reported favorably on this scheme and which led the floor fight for it.

When this reform failed to pass, the Young Turks turned on McGuire and stripped him of his powers, substantially as they had in 1894 and 1896. Again the rank and file rose to McGuire's defense, rejected every measure, and restored McGuire to his full preconvention powers. An immediate howl arose from the local leaders, but a recount sustained the results.

Once again the rank and file had rallied behind McGuire. But now they rallied around a name only. The person was hollow, the marrow all drained out, the fight gone. His old-fashioned, genteel, over-intellectualized, and quaint brand of utopian radicalism was as dead in 1901 as William McKinley, the Populist party, or the Knights of Labor. McGuire proceeded, like a faithful old dog, to die with the loyalties he had lived by.

Socialism and the
American Labor Movement

JOHN H. M. LASLETT

Among the exceptional features of the American labor movement, none has been more striking than its independence from the political Left. The "large" answers leap to mind—the lack of class consciousness, the responsiveness of the two-party system, the high wage levels, and so on. True as such explanations may be, they do not tell the whole story. Before World War I, the Socialists actually had a powerful hold in the movement: they controlled many important unions and, at their peak, mustered 40 percent of the vote at the AFL convention of 1912. How, in specific cases, can the decline from substantial power be explained? In this essay, John Laslett undertakes to analyze the failure through the experience of individual unions that had been socialist strongholds. His tentative conclusions suggest a historical process much more complex than what has traditionally been written on the subject. Yet one wonders whether it will yet be possible to reduce the complexity to a simple truth —along the lines, say, of the irrelevancy of the socialist influence: it could stay or go as it pleased so long as it did not interfere with the effective operations of trade unions, and so, having no function, ultimately subsided everywhere. There would then be the further question: What was there in pure-and-simple unionism that tolerated the socialists but so persistently required them to function on its terms?

I N A RECENT STUDY, PUBLISHED ELSEWHERE, I SUGGESTED THAT IN addition to the generally accepted sociological explanations for the failure of socialism in the American labor movement, such as the absence of a strong sense of class consciousness, the flexibility of the two-

From John H. M. Laslett, "Socialism and the American Labor Movement: Some New Reflections," *Labor History*, VIII (Spring, 1967), pp. 136–155. Reprinted by permission of the publisher. Footnotes have been omitted except where they amplify the text.

party system, or the high level of wages in the American economy, there was another factor which was also of considerable importance. This was the apparent fact that, despite their recognition of the need for militancy and democracy in the trade union movement, and their emphasis on broadening its base by organizing the unskilled and semi-skilled workers, the socialists pursued policies in the trade unions themselves that proved, in practice, to be less successful in protecting the interests of workingmen than those followed by the more conservative business unionists.

This hypothesis was based upon a contrast, in the years 1886 to 1900, between the successful job-conscious unionism of the Cigarmakers' International Union and the apparent failure of the policies pursued by two socialist-controlled organizations: the Bakers' and Confectioners' International Union and the Boot and Shoe Workers' Union. This sample was a small one, covering a limited period of time, and the conclusions drawn from it were therefore put forward in a very tentative manner. The purpose of the present study is to re-examine the initial hypothesis in the context of the later period of socialist influence of the A.F.L., which lasted from 1900 until after the First World War. It should be emphasized at the outset that the discussion deals primarily with only two international unions, so that whatever conclusions emerge must again be considered provisional. Nevertheless, it is hoped that they will prove useful to students of the subject generally.

Before examining socialist policies in the post-1900 A.F.L., it is necessary to summarize more fully the results of my previous study. The job-conscious craft unionism of the A.F.L., as manifested in the Cigarmakers' International Union, concerned itself primarily (as did organizations of skilled workmen in England and elsewhere) with an attempt to provide job security for union members by means of high dues and large financial reserves, an extensive benefit system, and strong central union control, especially in the use of the strike weapon. These economic policies were supplemented by a nonpartisan political policy, based on the familiar A.F.L. program of "reward your friends, punish your enemies," which was intended to secure state and federal legislation favorable to the interests of union members. From the economic point of view, these policies did in fact do much to bring stability and success to the Cigarmakers' Union —it was, for instance, one of the few unions to come through the major depression of the 1890s largely unscathed—so that by 1900 it had grown from a small, weak organization into one of the largest and most successful of the craft unions in the A.F.L. Politically, after numerous vicissitudes the Cigarmakers managed to secure a law from the New York State Assembly banning the use of tenement buildings for cigar manufacture, by lobbying and by voting for the candidates of either major political party who were willing to give the legislation their support.

In the Bakers' and the Boot and Shoe Workers' unions, however, where the socialists were influential, different policies were pursued. In both of these unions the socialist leadership kept union dues low, on the ground that high dues prevented many of the poorer workers, who could not afford them, from being organized. They held the benefit systems and larger treasuries undermined the militancy of union organizations and turned them into mere benefit societies. And they considered strict methods of control over strikes to be unfair and undemocratic, arguing instead for a greater degree of local autonomy.[1] In politics, both unions repudiated the nonpartisan methods of the A.F.L. as a betrayal of the workers' class interests, and gave their support instead to one or another of the workingmen's parties in existence at this time, most notably to the Socialist Labor Party (S.L.P.).

This general position was in fact maintained by many of the more militant socialists in the A.F.L. for a number of years. But in both the Bakers' and the Boot and Shoe Workers' unions it soon became apparent that these policies were unable to provide union members either with economic security or with protective legislation to the same extent that the leading craft unions seemed able to do. Without high dues or a strong treasury, the leaders of the Bakers' and the Boot and Shoe Workers' unions could do little to improve the wages or conditions of work of the membership. During the depression of the 1890s the Bakers' Union—unlike the Cigarmakers' Union—had to borrow to remain solvent; and the bargaining position of the Boot and Shoe Workers' Union was so weak that its membership continued to fall, even after the depression was over.

Politically, too, both these unions found that if they were to secure legislation favorable to their interests it was inexpedient to give their undivided support to the S.L.P. In 1893 bakers in California secured a six-day work week by lobbying in the state legislature; and in 1895 the New York locals of the union gave their support to a Republican candidate for the state Assembly because of his efforts on behalf of a bake-shop law.

Soon after this both unions adopted high dues and benefits, overhauled

---

[1] The degree to which unions favored high dues, benefit systems, and central control also depended, of course, on the level of wages in the industry, the availability of alternative benefit societies, and the size of the product market. But socialists often advocated low dues, fewer benefits, and local autonomy on ideological grounds, irrespective of these other factors.

their internal structure, and whilst remaining radical in politics for a number of years brought their general policies much closer to the prevailing philosophy of the A.F.L. As a result, the position of both generally improved. By 1903 the Bakers' Union had a surplus in its treasury and a membership of 18,000; and by 1904 the downward trend in the fortunes of the Boot and Shoe Workers' Union had been so successfully reversed that it had over 60,000 members on its books. These years were a period of general prosperity, in which all unions prospered, but it seems clear that the policy changes of these two unions played a considerable part in their development and growth.

It seems clear, on the basis of this evidence at least, that in the period before 1900 there was a sharp dichotomy between the socialist view of trade union policy and the A.F.L. view; and that it was the A.F.L. view which proved to be the more successful. It is also clear, however, that the socialist movement in the 1890s was dominated by the DeLeonites, who were bitterly opposed to the craft union policies of the A.F.L., but who even at this time by no means represented socialist opinion as a whole. Moderate Socialists, led by Debs, Berger, Hillquit and others, were skeptical of the trade union policies pursued by the S.L.P., and in 1898 they broke with DeLeon. Three years later they helped to found the Socialist Party of America, which specifically recognized the importance of economic trade unionism and repudiated the "impossibilist" tactics of the DeLeonites.

At its founding convention, held in Indianapolis in July 1901, the Socialist Party adopted a resolution offering friendship and support to the trade union movement, and urged socialists, as a matter of duty, to "assist in building up and unifying the trades and labor organizations." On the matter of political action, the convention stated that although individual trade unionists were to be encouraged to join the Socialist Party, it was recognized that trade unions as such were "by historical necessity organized on neutral grounds, as far as political affiliation is concerned." These views were reaffirmed at subsequent conventions of the party.

Thus the Socialist Party, unlike the Socialist Labor Party, was officially committed to a policy of support for the existing trade union movement. In practice, of course, there were frequent disputes on the issue. There were those, on the left of the party, who remained firmly opposed to the job-conscious trade unionism of the A.F.L., regarding it as a reactionary organization to which no support should be given. There were those, including Debs, who favored a combination of industrial unionism and socialist political action, a position which led them to give their support to the I.W.W. for a brief period after 1905. Still others were indifferent to the trade union movement and wished to concentrate instead on building up the Socialist Party as a political organization seeking state and national office. The result of all this was that after 1900 the socialists pursued a variety of policies within the trade union movement which in part confirm the conclusions suggested about socialist-trade union relations before 1900, but which also require substantial modifications to them.

In the period between 1900 and the years immediately following the First World War there were many unions in the A.F.L. in which the socialists were influential. They remained strong in unions controlled by radical immigrants, such as the Brewers' Union, in industrial organizations, such as the United Mine Workers of America, and a number of craft unions also, such as the Boot and Shoe Workers' Union, to which reference has already been made. The two unions in which their influence was perhaps at its most characteristic, however—reflecting both the immigrant and the indigenous elements in American socialism—were the International Ladies' Garment Workers' Union, and the International Association of Machinists. These were two of the largest and most important organizations in the A.F.L., and from 1900 until after the First World War they were either strongly influenced or controlled by socialists of one kind or another. By 1926, however, socialist influence in both of them had largely disappeared, although it persisted longer among the garment workers than among the machinists. It is worthwhile to examine the reasons for the decline of socialism in both these unions for the light which it throws upon the fortunes of the socialists in the trade union movement in general.

The International Ladies' Garment Workers' Union, founded in New York City in 1900, did not become really influential until 1909-10 with the success of two major strikes in the cloak and shirtwaist trades. Then it grew rapidly, dominated by a relatively small number of large locals in New York, and characterized by great militancy in both its industrial and its political activities, and by a progressive attitude towards the social welfare of its members. It had a semi-industrial structure, frequently incorporating several different kinds of workers into a single local, and at first it consisted largely of Jewish immigrants from Russia and from Eastern Europe, many of whom had been active in revolutionary movements there. It was these factors, coupled with the seasonal nature of the garment trade and the low wages and bad conditions of the sweatshops, which account for its persistently radical stand.

The International Association of Machinists, by contrast, was an organization of skilled workers, many of them railroad machinists who were American born or immigrants of long standing, which grew steadily from its southern origins in 1888 to become a large and nationally organized trade union. Its socialism was more moderate than that of the Ladies' Garment Workers' and to a greater extent reflected the indigenous traditions of American reform. It derived partly from the influence of Debs and his plans for industrial unionism on the railroads, and partly from the more radical elements within the Knights of Labor and the Populist movement, both of which were influential in the southern and midwestern states where the union first developed. More important than either of these factors, however, were the effects of rapid mechanization on the machinists' trade, which undermined their skill, created considerable redundancy, and turned many machinists from independent artisans into shop and factory hands.

In both the Machinists' and the Ladies' Garment Workers' unions there was, at least at first, considerable evidence of the kind of "impossibilist" tactics which had characterized the socialist movement of the 1890s. The Machinists' Union was not socialist to begin with, and between 1893 and 1912 it developed, under the leadership of James O'Connell, most of the policies associated with the business unionism of the A.F.L.: a strong treasury, a well developed benefit system, and a widespread system of contracts with employers. For some time the socialists in the Machinists' Union opposed these policies, even if they did so in more muted terms than the DeLeonites had used. They opposed the increases in per capita tax which were made by the 1905 and 1909 conventions, and in 1910 caused the administration considerable financial embarrassment by securing the repeal of a provision for an annual assessment which had earlier been passed. In an address to the convention of 1911 the leader of the socialist faction, William H. Johnston, attacked the assessment method of raising funds, and asserted that broadening the union's membership was much more important than raising its dues. "It would not make any great difference," he said, ". . . if we had ten million dollars in our treasury and only the limited number of members that we now have." This attitude was part of a general campaign on the part of the socialists to transform the organization from a craft into an industrial union and to unite the machinists, together with other trade unionists, into a single federation of the metal trades. There was also socialist criticism of the tendency towards centralization which occurred in O'Connell's administration.

A similar kind of conflict took place in this period in the Ladies' Garment Workers' Union, although the garment industry was quite different from the machinists' trade, and the climate of opinion in the union considerably further to the left. Here the debate took place, not between a conservative administration and a socialist minority, but between an administration controlled by moderate socialists, on the one hand, and a group of radical insurgents, on the other. The Ladies' Garment Workers' Union was led by socialists from the very beginning, but General Secretary-Treasurer John A. Dyche and other union leaders, faced with a rapidly changing labor force and serious organizing problems due to the seasonal nature of the trade, strove hard to stabilize the union and give it permanence by advocating many of the economic policies which had proved successful in the other unions of the A.F.L. In its early years the union had low dues, few financial reserves, and—because the bulk of its membership was concentrated in a relatively few local unions in New York City—a loose-knit structure which gave the larger locals a great deal of autonomy, particularly in the matter of strikes.

Dyche and President Rosenberg made frequent attempts to remedy this situation, but with little success: in his report to the 1912 union convention, Dyche said that "as long as our locals . . . enjoy, as they do now, almost complete autonomy and our present Per Capita . . . from which members get no more than moral support in cases of need [remains the same], then our International Union, however large its membership may be at any time, will never be more, to put it bluntly and frankly, than a paper organization." Nevertheless the administration succeeded, after the major strikes of 1910, in securing the celebrated Protocol of Peace, a collective agreement signed with the Manufacturers' Protective Association in New York which did much to stabilize the trade in the city and which was, in its provisions for regulating future disputes, virtually unique at the time.

The radicals in the Ladies' Garment Workers' Union who opposed these changes were the younger, more recently arrived immigrants who had little experience of trade unionism and who brought with them a zeal for political action derived from their part in the revolutionary movement of Czarist Russia. They were influenced also by the failure of numerous attempts to establish a stable trade union in the women's garment industry in the early days, and by the "direct action" philosophy of the syndicalists, which helped to give the I.W.W. a certain influence in the needle trades. Thus they opposed efforts to raise the union's dues and establish a permanent strike benefit and, in the celebrated Hourwich affair of 1913, displayed considerable hostility towards the Protocol of Peace. Initially, this dispute arose over the personal role which Dr. Isaac Hourwich played as chief negotiator for the New York Joint Board of Cloakmakers' Unions, but it soon raised issues concerned with autonomy, with strike policy, and with relations to employers in general which developed into an attack on the Protocol as such. The union had conceded the right to strike in return for the machinery established for regulating disputes, and the radicals, chafing under this and other restrictions of the Protocol, denounced the union leaders as "fakers, traitors, partners with the bosses, [and] reactionaries," in much the same terms that the De-Leonites had used.

It seems clear, therefore, that at least some of the more militant social-ists in the trade union movement continued to pursue "impossibilist" tactics for a considerable time after 1900, reflecting the generally hostile attitude towards the A.F.L. of the radical wing of the Socialist Party. But as time went on, the socialists in the Machinists' and the Ladies' Garment Workers' Unions modified their critical attitude towards A.F.L. trade unionism, although they never quite abandoned it altogether. It has been shown that the moderate socialist leadership in the Ladies' Garment Workers' Union favored strong trade union policies from the first. But even the more radical socialists, as they acquired greater influence in the union, became willing to retain and to expand the economic policies which had been set going under Dyche and Rosenberg. To remove the bitterness which had been generated by the Hourwich affair, a new ad-ministration headed by Benjamin Schlesinger was elected in 1914. In an editorial in the union journal soon after he was elected Schlesinger, while reassuring the radicals that many of their complaints against the Protocol had been justified, made it clear that his administration would continue the Protocol as the most practicable way of adjusting the union's relations with the employers. And when the Protocol finally did break down in 1915, to be replaced by a more conventional trade agreement, it was be-cause the Protocol was no longer found to be useful, not because of any repudiation of trade agreements as such.

The Schlesinger administration also tried to reduce the number of un-authorized shop strikes and continued the campaign to raise the union's per capita and establish a strike benefit fund, which was considered essential if the union was to expand its activities beyond New York and a few other major garment centers. In 1916 the weekly dues paid to the International were raised from $2\frac{1}{2}$ to 4 cents per week, and by 1924 this had been increased to 15 cents. On the issue of local autonomy versus central control, the Schlesinger administration favored increasing the powers of the general officers *vis-à-vis* the Joint Boards and the giant locals in New York. It also encouraged local unions to expand their sick and death benefits, and was responsible for the development of other measures for the welfare of union members, notably the Union Health Center. But it is noteworthy that the need for such measures was justified in terms of the idealistic and humanitarian traditions of the union, rather than in the commercial terms which were often used by the more con-servative craft unions.

Nor did these changes mean that the union abandoned its radical traditions, although there were some who believed that they did. "Among a large section of our membership," Schlesinger wrote in the *Ladies' Garment Worker* in August 1917, "the old notion is still prevalent that a big treasury is detrimental to the revolutionary spirit." But he argued that proper financial reserves would increase the chances for success in the strikes undertaken by the union, and that this would enhance the spirit of class solidarity instead of diminishing it. "With a large capital in our treasury and with true enthusiasm animating us our radicalism would bring us much further."

In the Machinists' Union the socialists also demonstrated that when faced with the responsibilities of power they accepted the need for a well-organized and financially strong trade union. A socialist administration, under William H. Johnston, was elected to office in 1912, and it continued most of the economic policies which had been set in motion under O'Connell. The per capita was raised by referendum vote in 1913, and in the following years further increases were made. The benefit system was also improved. A life insurance program was established in 1920 as a means of retaining the increased membership which entered the union during the First World War.

The powers of the Grand Lodge were also further developed, despite earlier socialist emphasis on decentralization and democracy. In 1916 the tenure of union officers was extended from two to four years, and in 1924 the semi-independent General Executive Board was replaced by a group of officials more directly under the President's control. The main purpose of these measures was to enable the union to resist increasing pressure from the employers, which reached a new peak in the years following the First World War. In addition to this, the failure of a major railroad shopmen's strike in 1922, in which many machinists were involved, and the open-shop campaign which followed it, forced the socialists to adopt a more conciliatory attitude towards the employers than they had had hitherto. This led to a policy of union-management cooperation, known as the Baltimore and Ohio plan, which brought greater collaboration between union and employers than existed in most other trades.

Thus although some socialists in the Machinists' and Ladies' Garment Workers' Unions persisted with "impossibilist" tactics in the period after 1900—a fact which continued to do the socialist cause considerable harm —most adopted the same general economic policies as the other trade unionists in the A.F.L. Nor can it be said, as it could with some plausibility be said of the 1890s, that socialist leadership in the post-1900 trade-union movement tended to bring failure rather than success. Under the Johnston administration, which lasted from 1912 to 1926, the Machinists' Union membership rose to a high of 331,449; and although the union suffered major setbacks after the First World War, this was of course also true of non-socialist unions. It does not seem in general that the Johnston administration achieved less for the machinists than the conservative O'Connell administration which preceded it.

The success of the Ladies' Garment Workers' Union was even more striking. Operating under socialist leadership throughout the entire period, it grew from a small, ineffective organization into one of the largest and most powerful unions in the A.F.L. It raised wages in the industry considerably, and did much to overcome the evils of the sweatshop. Like the Machinists' Union, it suffered setbacks after 1920, but again this was due to factors which affected the labor movement as a whole, not to any obvious defects in the leadership as such. It must be added, also, that much of this progress was achieved without the financial resources which many A.F.L. leaders considered essential for success. Despite the reforms of the Schlesinger administration, the Ladies' Garment Workers' Union rarely had enough money to finance its operations, and because of its semi-industrial structure the degree of internal discipline which characterized a number of A.F.L. craft unions was difficult to achieve.

Moreover, although the socialists in both the Machinists' and the Ladies' Garment Workers' unions adopted or maintained most of the prevailing economic policies of other American unions in the period, they also persisted with their independent political stand, at least for a time, despite the nonpartisan position taken by the majority of A.F.L. unions. Their position differed from the behavior of the Bakers and the Boot and Shoe Workers (in the DeLeonite period), which tended to de-emphasize radical politics once they had become established in the economic field.

Thus the socialists in the Machinists' Union criticized the nonpartisan political tactics of the A.F.L., opposed its policy of sending delegations to the Democratic and Republican party conventions, and did their best to promote the cause of the Socialist Party within their union. At the Machinists' convention of 1903 they made an unsuccessful attempt to commit the union to supporting the party, and in state and municipal elections between 1904 and 1910 machinists stood for local office on the socialist ticket in Illinois, New York, Wisconsin, and elsewhere. When the Johnston administration took office in 1912, the machinists gave their support to Debs and the socialist ticket generally in the presidential election of that year.

During the period of the First World War the Machinists' Union modified its socialist stand. In April 1915 the union journal acknowledged that the Clayton Act and other labor measures were due largely to the vigorous lobbying tactics of the A.F.L. and the railroad brotherhoods, although it still maintained that labor legislation would be easier to secure "when we select men from our own ranks to represent us." Nevertheless, after this the Machinists' Union became more and more sympathetic to Woodrow Wilson's administration, as did the trade unions generally. In 1916 it supported Wilson for re-election, and when the war came it endorsed his attempts to maintain proper standards for labor. The nationalization of the railroads had for years been the union's major political aim, and when Wilson took them under public control it was even more gratified.

But after the war, with the defeat of the Democrats and the election of a hostile Republican administration, the Machinists' Union returned for a time to its former radical stand. It was disillusioned by the restoration of the railroads to private ownership, and eagerly supported the Plumb Plan for their public control. When the Conference for Progressive Political Action (C.P.P.A.) was established in 1922, with nationalization of the railroads as one of its major aims, the Machinists' Union gave it full support. Johnston, moreover, was prominent among those labor leaders who tried to convert the C.P.P.A. from a nonpartisan organization into a political labor party. He became chairman of the conference, and made it clear in his speeches that he hoped the movement would "result in the creation of a new party, . . . in the workers marshalling their forces on the political field of action under a common banner for the purpose of electing their own representatives to our legislative bodies."

On this issue Johnston was now more radical than many of the other leaders of the Machinists' Union, who were less willing to take an independent course. Nevertheless, Johnston vigorously supported the nomination of La Follette for the presidency in 1924, and maintained his hope that the C.P.P.A. would turn into a new political party at least until the fall elections of that year. The defeat of La Follette and the growth of internal conflicts within the union, however, forced Johnston to abandon these hopes.

Although the Machinists' commitment to independent labor politics wavered after 1912, the Ladies' Garment Workers' Union gave its full support to the Socialist Party right up to the First World War and beyond. At the national level, it supported Debs and the other candidates of the party in virtually every election, giving them financial as well as electoral support. The union also gave money to a variety of radical causes, such as the Workmen's Circle, the Rand School of Social Science, and the amnesty campaign conducted after the war to free victims of the "Red Scare."

Co-operation between Socialist Party and the Ladies' Garment Workers' Union was particularly close at the local level, in New York City and elsewhere. The socialist press supported the union's efforts to improve the conditions of its members; Socialist Party locals raised money for the union during strikes; and Meyer London and Morris Hillquit, two of the party's most prominent national leaders, served successively as legal counsel for the union and its New York Cloakmakers Joint Board. In return the membership gave these men, and other socialist candidates for electoral office in New York, their wholehearted political support. Campaign committees of cloakmakers in the twelfth congressional district were largely responsible for electing London repeatedly to Congress, and similar efforts were made to help Hillquit in his various campaigns, notably in the mayoral election of 1917. Union members as such also ran for state and municipal office on the socialist ticket. Elmer Rosenberg, for instance, the First Vice-President, was a socialist member of the New York State Assembly for a number of years.

After 1920, when the Socialist Party had split and there were a number of groups contending for the leadership of the radical movement, many of the socialists in the Ladies' Garment Workers' Union pressed strongly for the establishment of a new, broadly-based labor party, based upon an alliance between the socialists and other labor groups. In this campaign they met resistance from some of the older socialists, who feared that such a coalition would bring a dilution of socialist principles. Nevertheless, the union welcomed the establishment of local workingmen's parties in various parts of the country, and helped to effect an electoral alliance between the New York branches of the National Farmer-Labor Party and the Socialist Party in the fall elections of 1922. It took a prominent part in the development of the C.P.P.A., and tried hard to convert it into a national labor party on the British model. It even maintained its support for a labor party after 1925, when the C.P.P.A. collapsed, although by now the cause was almost hopeless. As late as 1929 the union convention adopted a resolution reaffirming "the traditional support of our International in favor of the organization of a labor party," and it was not until the New Deal that the bulk of the membership finally switched to the Democrats.

In view of the considerable economic successes of the Machinists' and the Ladies' Garment Workers' unions, and their continued loyalty to the Socialist Party or to some form of independent political action right up to the First World War and beyond, it seems clearly an exaggeration to suggest that the policies pursued by the socialist trade unions were in general less successful in protecting the members' interests than these adopted by the more conservative unions. This is not to say that this hypothesis should be abandoned altogether. There is evidence that the increasing effectiveness of the political and the economic policies of the A.F.L. unions generally did help to diminish enthusiasm for socialism in both the Machinists' and the Ladies' Garment Workers' unions. In the matter of political action, for instance, as long as public ownership of the railroads was still an academic issue, the Machinists' Union held that the only way to secure public ownership was to elect a majority of socialists to Congress. But in 1920, when the union was alarmed by the return of the railroads to private hands after the wartime period of federal control, it adopted the A.F.L. policy of exerting pressure on individual congressmen in order to restore public control. "If we are to obtain beneficial legislation," wrote a leading official in the union journal, "we must play the game with the two old parties, using one against the other." In this case, and in any similar situation, it seems clear that the "reward your friends, punish your enemies" policy of the A.F.L. was the only course of action which had any chance of success.

As for economic action, Morris Hillquit in a speech to the 1924 convention of the Ladies' Garment Workers' Union showed clearly his regret that the success which the union had had in raising wages, improving conditions, and reducing hours, had undermined the radical sentiments which had been traditional amongst the membership. "It must never be forgotten," he said, "that the labor movement and your movement are not based solely on material struggles and material improvements. Of course, we want better material conditions; . . . but this is not the end. The labor movement is ever struggling for better and higher conditions of life, . . . for universal prosperity, and universal brotherhood, and for peace."

Nevertheless, the initial hypothesis put forward concerning the failure of socialism in the trade movement in the 1890s must clearly be supplemented by other factors when dealing with the period after 1900. One of these factors was undoubtedly the First World War and the "Red Scare" which followed it. The consequences of opposition to American participation in the war on the fortunes of the Socialist Party as a political organization are already well known. But it is important to notice the effects of this opposition on the position of the socialists in the trade unions, who were torn between their socialist convictions and their loyalty to the A.F.L., which gave full support to the war. In practice the socialists, at least those in the Machinists' and the Ladies' Garment Workers' unions, also endorsed the war, though not without misgivings; and although little was said about it this undoubtedly caused a number of trade unionists to sever their connections with the Socialist Party and with the left in general.

It was particularly difficult, for instance, for the Machinists' Union to maintain its radical stand, since it occupied an important place in the armaments industry and was fearful of being considered disloyal; and as the war went on the *Machinists' Journal* gave considerable publicity to the American Alliance for Labor and Democracy, the patriotic organization sponsored by the A.F.L. to counteract the anti-war activities of the socialists. But the same problem arose in the Ladies' Garment Workers' Union, which expressed considerable scepticism about the war until Germany's attacks upon Russia brought a serious threat to the country with which many garment workers still had personal or family ties. It then came out wholeheartedly for the conflict, and bought $100,000 of Liberty Bonds to demonstrate its loyalty.

Closely related to the war issue were the problems created by the Russian Revolution and the establishment of the American Communist Party. Despite general public opposition, both the Machinists' and the Ladies' Garment Workers' Unions supported the Russian Revolution, though the garment workers naturally did so with greater fervor since it brought the overthrow of the Czarist regime under which many of them had suffered. But when the Trade Union Educational League, under William Z. Foster, set up dual organizations in a number of trades in order to establish communist control, a serious conflict developed which further damaged the position of the left in the trade union movement as a whole.

The Johnston administration in the Machinists' Union was forced to rule that Communist Party membership was, in effect, inconsistent with union membership, despite the fact that the communists claimed to be promoting industrial unionism, which Johnston personally upheld. In the Ladies' Garment Workers' Union the conflict was even more serious, since the communists were far more numerous, and succeeded in capturing some of the largest and most important locals in New York. For years a bitter civil war was waged, and it was not until the 1930s that most of the communists had been successfully expelled. In both unions, however, the most important consequence of this conflict was the expulsion or withdrawal of large numbers of radicals—in the Ladies' Garment Workers' Union, many thousands—who had supplied these unions with much of their militant outlook. Added to this development was a strong feeling of disillusionment with the left in general, and a degree of preoccupation with internal problems which left these unions with little time or energy to devote to their traditional concern for the broader problems of the labor movement.

Another factor in the decline of socialism in these unions was the increasing irrelevance of many of the issues which had first led to radicalism. The Machinists' Union was composed largely of native Americans, and its radicalism derived primarily from American sources: the Knights of Labor, Populism, and hostility towards the railroads and the "monopoly power." But these elements in the populist tradition, though of great importance in the 1890s and early 1900s, had lost much of their appeal by the late 1920s. Similarly, in the Ladies' Garment Workers' Union, many of the issues which gave the union its revolutionary zeal at the turn of the century—the sweatshop, low wages, and the revolutionary traditions brought from Eastern Europe—had now lost much of their force, and most of the early generation of leaders had left the scene. The success of the Russian Revolution brought a renewal of the radical impulse but, as already indicated, the conflict which it engendered weakened the left wing in the unions instead of strengthening it.

Moreover, in addition to the desire to become assimilated into American society—and to adopt American political habits along with American citizenship—it was relatively easy for immigrant needle workers to set themselves up as garment manufacturers on their own, a factor which undoubtedly helped to undermine the socialist traditions of that union. And although other issues arose upon which to base a new radical movement, the New Deal effectively prevented it from taking an independent political form.

But perhaps more important than any of these reasons in explaining the decline of socialism in the trade union movement was the political weakness of socialism and the Socialist Party. For a time before the First World War, when the Socialist Party was still growing, there was something to be said for union members giving it their support. But after the war, when the Socialist Party had split and the left in general returned to the fragmented state which it had been in before 1900, there was little point in giving it political support. In unions such as the Ladies' Garment Workers' Union, where the revolutionary tradition was strong, a political labor party might still have been endorsed had there been any serious prospect of such a party being formed. But in less radical trade unions, such as the Machinists' Union, there was a growing conviction that the Socialist Party, or any similar organization, would never attract the political support of the bulk of American workingmen. A Pittsburgh leader of the Machinists' Union perhaps put it best when he wrote in the *Machinists' Monthly Journal* in April 1920: "The Socialists have claimed for years to be the party of the workers, . . . yet the workers will not or have not joined hands with them, which leads me to think the worker is not a party man, or to put it another way, the worker can be counted on as being a non-partisan voter."

It is not suggested that this is a complete analysis of the reasons for the failure of socialism in the American trade union movement. As indicated at the outset, the sample dealt with here is a small one, and in any event a review of the tactics followed by particular trade unions does not take adequate account of the many other ethnic, social, and political factors which were also involved. Although reference has been made to some of these factors, a much more extended analysis of them is necessary before any firm conclusions can be drawn.

Nevertheless, the evidence does suggest that socialism did not fail in the A.F.L. simply because of the success of "pure and simple" trade unionism, as was suggested some years ago by Charles A. Gulick and Melvin K. Bers of the University of California. There is evidence for this view, and it is likely that in the long run the increasing affluence which successful business unionism made possible helped to undermine the radical traditions of the socialist trade unions. But there were clearly other factors at work, and the willingness of some socialist unions to pursue independent labor politics for some time *after* they had become successful in the economic field indicates that, had political conditions been right, they might well have continued to support the idea of an independent labor party, at least for a time. The experience of the labor movement throughout much of Europe, and particularly in England, in the late nineteenth and early twentieth centuries indicates that there was no necessary conflict between radical politics and the traditional economic objectives of trade unionism.

Nor is it quite fair to say, as Professor Daniel Bell has suggested, that excessive preoccupation with an extremist ideology was the major reason why the socialists failed. Although some of the socialists in them continued to follow "impossibilist" tactics throughout, at least in regard to the two unions considered here, the evidence suggests that there was flexibility when it came to the practical issues confronting the labor movement as a whole.

The problem facing the socialists in the A.F.L. was the same as that of any radical minority trying to convert a majority to its side. To adopt a doctrinaire revolutionary position, such as the DeLeonites in the 1890s and later the communists attempted to do, alienated the trade union leadership and ignored most of the relevant facts about American society. It was more sensible to pursue a moderate course, as the Socialist Party did, adopting many of the trade union policies of the A.F.L. but maintaining an independent political stand. Despite this, the socialists still failed to attract more than a small minority of trade unionists to their side. This was in part due to the success of "pure and simple" trade unionism. But it was also due to the more general factors which have traditionally prevented the growth of a successful socialist movement in America.

The Origins of Western
Working Class Radicalism

MELVYN DUBOFSKY

Both John R. Commons and Selig Perlman, the principal exponents of the Wisconsin school of labor history, identified the frontier as one of the keys to American labor conservatism: Westward expansion and land availability generated a sense of optimism and opportunity that militated against class consciousness and labor radicalism. Yet, paradoxically, it was also true that the West was the site of the one brand of American unionism that was authentically radical. At the very time that the American Federation of Labor was embarking on its "pure-and-simple" course, events in the West were leading to the formation in 1905 of the Industrial Workers of the World. What caused this reversal of form in one section of the country? In this essay Melvyn Dubofsky, author of a major new history of the IWW (*We Shall Be All*), attempts to find an answer in the forces acting on the western working class. He rejects the notion that frontier conditions—the equalitarian streak and the easy resort to violence—begot labor radicalism. On the contrary, Dubofsky argues that the radical impulse was triggered by the swift arrival of full-fledged corporate capitalism in the hard-rock mining industry. The blatant alliance of corporate interests and public authorities also turned western workers violently against the standing order. Finally, there was a western radical tradition that went back to the Knights of Labor and the Populists. Persuasive as are his lines of arguments, Dubofsky's case will remain inconclusive until there is an answer to the further question: To what extent were the foregoing conditions distinctive to the West?

From Melvyn Dubofsky, "The Origins of Working Class Radicalism, 1890–1905," *Labor History,* VII (Spring, 1966), pp. 131–154. Reprinted by permission of the publisher. Footnotes have been omitted except where they amplify the text.

FIFTY YEARS AGO THE LABOR ECONOMIST AND HISTORIAN LOUIS Levine (Lorwin) explained the origins of the radical unionism and syndicalism which the Lawrence textile strike of 1912 had brought to the American nation's attention. Rather than viewing American syndicalism as the product of a few inspired individuals or as a sudden decision to imitate French ideas and methods, Levine insisted that working-class radicalism could only be understood by a proper examination of United States economic and political developments. He wrote: "The forces which drove American toilers to blaze new paths, to forge new weapons and to reinterpret the meaning of life in new terms were the struggle and compromises, the adversities and successes, the exultation and despair *born of conditions of life in America."* Unfortunately, in the half century since Levine's seminal article, too few historians have chosen to investigate his hypothesis. The field has been left to labor economists more concerned with the nature of industrial relations and the internal history of individual trade unions than with the dynamics of historical change. This paper will apply the historical method and research into unused or seldom used documents to analyze the forces which impelled the working class in a part of the American West to adopt socialism and syndicalism.

At the outset several concepts require clarification. By the American West, I mean the metals-mining area stretching from the northern Rockies to the Mexican border, and particularly the states of Colorado, Idaho, and Montana. By radicalism, I mean, not murder or mayhem, but a concept of social change and a program for altering the foundations of American society and government, which was proscripted ultimately from the Marxian indictment of capitalism. This paper makes no pretense, however, of offering an exegesis on the theoretical foundations of Western working-class radicalism or of its decline and fall; instead it simply seeks to comprehend why, within a particular historical, social, and economic context, a group of American workers found radicalism relevant.

During the Populist and Progressive eras (1890–1917) when radicalism took root among Western workers, reform crusades—middle-class and lower-class, urban and rural, moderate and militant, conservative and revolutionary—challenged the classic capitalist order. This order, described fifty years earlier by Marx and Engels, was dying throughout the industrial world, the United States included; and social groups struggled to control or shape the economic order to come. None were sure of the future, but all wanted it to accord with their concept of a just and good society. In America many options *appeared* to exist, for in 1890 and 1900 the triumph of the modern corporation and the corporate state was still in the future. And Western workers were among those Americans who opted for an alternative to the capitalist order.

At this time the American Federation of Labor, with its conservatism and "pure and simple" policies, dominated organized labor. Its original competitor, the Knights of Labor, had declined and died; Populism had failed to cement a farmer-labor alliance; and in the East the immigrant needle trades workers had not yet built stable, semi-industrial, socialist organizations offering an alternative to the AFL craft unions. Western workers, however, presented a direct and radical challenge to AFL hegemony. Around the Western Federation of Miners (W.F.M.) rallied America's radical dissidents, those dissatisfied with things as they were —with McKinley, Roosevelt, Bryan and the political parties they represented, with Samuel Gompers and craft unionism, and especially with corporate capitalism.

Nowhere was the economic and social change which produced American radicalism in the late nineteenth century so rapid and so unsettling as in the mining West. There, in a short time, full-blown industrial cities replaced frontier boom-camps and substantially capitalized corporations displaced grub-staking prospectors. The profitable mining of refractory ores (silver and gold) and base metals (lead, zinc, and copper) required railroads, advanced technology, large milling and smelting facilities, and intensive capitalism. "The result," in the words of Rodman Paul, "was that [by 1880] many mining settlements were carried well beyond any stage of society that could reasonably be called the frontier. They became, instead, industrial islands in the midst of forest, desert, or mountain. . . ." During the 1890s and 1900s, with continuing economic growth, mining communities moved still further beyond the frontier stage. Corporations such as William Rockefeller's Amalgamated Copper Company and the Phelps-Dodge Company consolidated the copper industry; other large corporations exploited the lead and silver mines; and the American Smelting and Refining Company and the United States Reduction and Refining Company apparently monopolized the refining and smelting of ores.

As early as 1876, Colorado, though still sparsely settled and far removed from the nation's primary industrial centers, had been colonized by corporations and company towns. In Leadville, for example, the population increased from 200 in 1877 to 14,820 in 1880, by which time Leadville was a primary smelting center. Cripple Creek, the famous Colorado gold camp, surpassed Leadville. Beginning in 1892 when it was hidden in the wilderness, the Cripple Creek region changed overnight into an industrial fortress. By 1900 Cripple Creek advertised its 10,000 inhabitants, three railroads connecting the region to the outer world, and trolleys and electric lights serving the district's own needs. Domestic and foreign capital rushed to exploit Colorado's opportunities. Between 1893 and 1897, 3,057 new mining corporations were organized, each of which was capitalized at over one million dollars. By 1895 all Colorado's larger cities boasted mining exchanges, and the Colorado Springs Mining Exchange handled over 230 million mining shares valued at over $34 million in 1899.

Montana followed the Colorado pattern. Its production of ores, valued at $41 million in 1889, made it the nation's leading mining state. Butte, the copper capital by that time, had a population of 30,000, three banks with deposits in excess of $3,000,000, an adequate public school system, four hospitals, two fire companies, newspapers, and water, gas, and electric companies. Its wealthier classes lived in elegant homes and worked in handsome business residences; its miners and mill-men received over $500,000 monthly in wages, and over 100 smoke stacks poured out their residue night and day in what was hardly a frontier environment. Idaho, on a lesser scale, repeated Montana's and Colorado's development.

In their mill and smelter towns, their shoddy company houses and stores, their saloons, and their working class populations, the cities of the Mountain West bore a distinct resemblance to their Eastern industrial counterparts. The speed of the transition from a primitive to a more mature economy, from the village to the city, combined with the great instability of a mining economy, had important social consequences. Rapid economic growth, instead of bringing prosperity and contentment, brought unrest, conflict, violence, and radicalism.

Those workers who filled the young industrial cities of the West shared a tradition of union organization, a common language, and a certain amount of ethnic similarity. Miners had organized unions by the 1860s on the Comstock Lode. When that area's mines played out, its miners moved on to new lodes in Idaho, Colorado, and Montana, carrying the union idea with them. While in some mining districts the foreign-born outnumbered the native Americans, no great ethnic division separated foreigners from natives. In most mining communities the dominant foreign nationalities were of Irish, English (mostly Cornishmen), and Canadian extraction. The foreign-born, particularly the Cornishmen (better known as "Cousin Jacks") and the Irishmen, were professional miners, and many of their native American counterparts had forsaken prospecting and striking it rich for the steadier returns of wage labor. Furthermore, the Western mining centers shared with mining communities throughout the world the group solidarity derived from relative physical isolation and dangerous, underground work.

At first, owing largely to the ethnic composition of Western mining communities and to the reliance of local merchants and professionals upon the patronage of miners, workers and local businessmen were not split into hostile camps. Local businessmen and farmers often supported the miners in their struggle for union recognition and higher wages. In Idaho's mineral-rich Coeur d'Alene, the local inhabitants—farmer and merchant, journalist and physician, public official and skilled worker— sympathized with striking miners. A leading Idaho attorney and Democratic politician, Boise's James H. Hawley, from 1892 to 1894 defended indicted strikers, referred to them as friends and allies, and importuned President Cleveland to provide several with patronage positions. East of the Continental Divide in Montana, mine and smelter owners, battling among themselves, wooed their labor forces with promises of union recognition, higher wages, the eight-hour day, and improved working conditions. And even Bill Haywood admitted that in Colorado's Cripple Creek district prior to the 1903-04 civil war, miners and businessmen associated with each other, belonged to the same fraternal societies, and were bound together by ethnic ties.

Into these urban communities the modern corporation intruded to disrupt the local peace and to drive a wedge between the workers and their non-working class allies. The 1890s was an uneasy decade for American businesses, and for none more so than mining, milling, and smelting enterprises. The falling price of silver, the depression of 1893, the repeal of the Sherman Silver Purchase Act, and the inherent instabilities of extractive industries made mine owners and smelter operators anxious to reduce production costs and consequently less tolerant of labor's demands. Mining corporations formed associations to pressure railroads by threatening to close down mining properties and cease shipments until rates declined. But capitalists found it easier to make the necessary savings by substituting capital for labor.

Technological innovations increased productivity, but in so doing diluted labor skills and disrupted traditional patterns of work. While technological change did not as a rule decrease total earnings, it tended to lower piece rates and to reduce some formerly skilled workers to unskilled laborers (and thus lowered their earnings). Since the mining enterprises competed in a common market, all the Western mining areas experienced similar pressures on piece rates and established skills. In Bill Haywood's hyperbolic words: "There was no means of escaping from the gigantic force that was relentlessly crushing all of them beneath its cruel heel. The people of these dreadful mining camps were in a fever of revolt. There was no method of appeal; strike was their only weapon."

Thus in 1892 Coeur d'Alene miners revolted against technological change, corporate concentration, and a recently organized Mine Owners' Association. Supported by local citizens, the community's newspapers, and local officials, miners appeared on the verge of success when their capitalist opponents, aided by state and federal authorities, outflanked them. Federal troops crushed the labor revolt, imprisoning union leaders and prominent non-union local residents alike. Strike leaders, while awaiting trial in prison, brooded about their recent experiences and the future of Western mining communities. Then and there in an Idaho prison, they decided to create a new labor organization, joining together the separate miners' unions in Idaho, Montana, Colorado, California, Nevada, and the Southwestern territories. Upon their release from prison, they called a convention, which met in Butte in 1893 and established the Western Federation of Miners.

By 1893 the mining West, as shown above, had passed well beyond the frontier stage and the working class' emerging radicalism was hardly the response of pioneer individualists to frontier conditions. The W.F.M. did not consist mostly of men who had been prospectors and frontiersmen; it was not "permeated with the independent and often lawless spirit of the frontier"; nor did its radicalism result from a lack of respect for the social distinctions of a settled community, or a disregard by labor for the "elementary amenities of civilized life," or the absence of farmers, a neutral middle class, and others who might keep matters within bounds. Perlman and Taft, and their disciples, have in fact reversed the dynamics of social change in the Mountain West. The violent conflicts which they so fully described came, not on an undeveloped Western frontier but in a citadel of American industrialism and financial capitalism. Perlman's and Taft's "class war without a class ideology" resulted from a process of social polarization not from an absence of middle groups, and consequently brought Marxian class consciousness. After 1910 farmers and others did not suddenly settle the area to blur sharp class distinctions and end the class war. The Ludlow Massacre occurred in 1914, Butte erupted into violent industrial warfare from 1914–17, and the bitter Colorado County coal wars developed still later—in the 1920s.

Violent conflict came not from the "general characteristics of the frontier" or "quick on the trigger" employers and employees but from the general nature of early industrialism.[1] Western working-class history is

---

[1] It seems strange to seek to explain violent conflict in the Mountain West in Turnerian terms when at the very same time in the "settled, civilized" East, open warfare prevailed at Homestead, in Chicago during the Pullman Strike, and even later in Lawrence, Massachusetts and Paterson, New Jersey. It seems equally foolish to account for the creation (in the Mountain West) of private armies in frontier terms, when Eastern employers and even workers did likewise. The coal and iron police appeared in Pennsylvania, not Montana; Colorado employers and workers may have utilized Western "desperados" and gunmen but employers and workers in New York's garment industry made ample use of similar services provided by the metropolis' gun-slingers and club wielders. Such violence and conflict, wherever it erupted, seems more a characteristic of the early stages of industrialism than of any peculiar geographical environment.

the story not of the collapse of social polarization but of its creation. Prior to the triumph of corporate capitalism, Western workers retained numerous allies among local merchants, professionals, farmers, and party politicians. The interesting historical feature is the manner in which corporate executives separated labor from its quondam allies, and polarized society and politics to the disadvantage of the worker. The remainder of this paper will demonstrate that class war in the West created a class ideology, and that that ideology was Marxist because the Mountain West from 1890 to 1905 followed the classic Marxian pattern of development.

☆ ☆ ☆

The Westerners' radicalism derived quite directly and naturally from the forces which had successfully refashioned American society. Together with other individuals and groups forced by corporate capitalism to the bottom of the economic and social ladder, miners asserted their claim to a more decent treatment and a better place in the American system. They joined the Knights of Labor, crusaded with the Populists, and eventually united with Eastern socialists. Western workers wedded to the utopianism of the Knights, allured by the promises of Populism, and victimized by the corporation could not rest content with the "pure and simple" unionism of Samuel Gompers.

The local miners' unions which coalesced to form the W.F.M. in many cases had simply dropped their Knights of Labor affiliation without shedding the Knights' essential spirit and carried with them the fundamental ideal of the Knights, "the unity of all workers." Although many miners may have joined the Knights of Labor simply to gain better conditions or job security, many certainly became imbued with that organization's spirit of solidarity and its antipathy to capitalism. While the Knights vanished in the East, their organization had a marked rebirth in the Mountain West. Montana labor papers reported in 1894 that their State's Knights of Labor were advancing at a rate not attained in years and were ready to lead laborers into the Populist crusade. On the other side of the Bitterroot range in Idaho, former Grand Master Workman, J. R. Sovereign, editor and publisher of the Wallace *Tribune*—the Coeur d'Alene miners' union official publication—was amalgamating the Knights, Populism, and the W.F.M. As late as 1903 a W.F.M. member from Slocan, B. C., wrote to the *Miners' Magazine:* "Now there are thousands of oldline K. of L.'s in the W.F. of M. and the unsavory acts of the A.F. of L. officials have not been all together forgotten. . . ."

W.F.M. members learned their political lessons in Populist schools. Unlike other areas of the nation where Populism was primarily an agrarian protest and labor, organized and unorganized, declined overtures from farm organizations for a political alliance, Populism in the Mountain West was a working-class movement and labor organizations courted farmers. Thus politics and Populism intruded at the early conventions of the W.F.M. The 1893 founding convention, meeting before panic and depression swept the West, considered the necessity of united political action. The 1895 convention, convened during the depths of depression, gave its endorsement and ". . . undivided support to the party [Populist] advocating the principles contained in the Omaha platform." Mining districts across the Mountain West elected miners' candidates to local office on labor or Populist tickets. And on occasion working-class Populists held the balance of power in statewide elections. Western miners, like farmers elsewhere, learned that politics paid.

Although free silver was obviously an important Populist attraction in the Mountain West, miners, unlike their employers, demanded sweeping political and economic reforms. If free silver had been the only manifestation of Western working-class political radicalism, it could have found an outlet in the Republican or Democratic parties as well as the People's party. The western workers instead supported a radical Populism —sometimes cranky, sometimes funny—which was the industrial counterpart of C. Vann Woodward's Southern Alliancemen and Norman Pollack's Midwestern agrarians. Consequently, after the failure of the Populist coalition with Silver Democrats and the defeat of Bryan, W.F.M. president Ed Boyce, speaking at the union's 1897 convention, denounced the free silver fraud and informed his audience: "The silver barons of the west are as bitter enemies of organized labor as the gold bug Shylock in his gilded den on Wall Street. . . ." Boyce then called for more intelligent and effective political action, a call which could lead in only one direction —toward the Socialist party. As the AFL turned away from socialism and political action to the narrower path of "pure and simple" trade unionism, the Western Federation moved toward socialism, political action, and the broad road of radical unionism.

Initially, however, the W.F.M., except for its unusual concern with Populism and politics, appeared much like any other trade union. It waged strikes to protect wages, reduce hours, or gain union recognition, not for the co-operative commonwealth. So famous an American radical as "Big Bill" Haywood, during his early years as an officer of the Silver City, Idaho local, concerned himself not with the coming revolution but with enrolling all working miners in the union. Nowhere do the minute books of Haywood's local, which he kept, hint of a future revolutionist. Ed Boyce, the union leader most responsible for transforming the W.F.M. into the cynosure of left-wing socialists, initially bore no taint of radicalism. During its first four years, 1893-1896, the W.F.M. seemed a rather ordinary trade union waging a losing battle against corporations and depression; in 1896 the organization was weaker and numbered fewer members than at its birth in 1893. Then the W.F.M. revived. And with apparent success came not conservatism or self-satisfaction but radicalism and revolutionary ardor.

The W.F.M.'s radicalism was buried deep in the organization's conscious and unconscious past. The Knights of Labor had contained an obvious utopian tinge; Populism, while less utopian, nevertheless proposed for the America of the 1890s a meaningful radical alternative. Many miners remained at heart Knights and Populists. Given the proper circumstances and the necessary motivation, both strains came alive in the W.F.M. The Western Federation transformed the naive idealism of the Knights and the native radicalism of the Populists into a brand of radicalism shared by socialist workers throughout the industrial world.

The Western Federation began as an open, inclusive union and became more so. "Open our portals to every workingman, whether engineer, blacksmith, smelterman, or millman . . . ," President Boyce advised the union convention in 1897. "The mantle of fraternity is sufficient for all." Three years later Boyce expanded his concept of fraternity: "We will at all times and under all conditions espouse the cause of the producing masses, regardless of religion, nationality or race, with the object of arousing them from the lethargy into which they have sunk, and which makes them willing to live in squalor. . . ." With Boyce and the W.F.M., commitment to solidarity and fraternity became more than platform oratory; the Western organization epitomized in philosophy and practice the spirit of industrial unionism.

Boyce's presidency also established economic and political radicalism as union policy. In his presidential inaugural speech, he directly challenged Gompers' approach to industrial relations and working-class organization. Speaking of his experience at the 1896 AFL convention, Boyce remarked: ". . . surely it is time for workingmen to see that trades unionism is a failure."

One might well ask, as Samuel Gompers himself wondered, what prompted the leader of a growing labor union to declare trade unionism a failure. And the answer might be that Boyce arrived at his conclusion not on theoretical or philosophical grounds but on the basis of the miners' union's actual experience in dealing with corporations. Even before the W.F.M. appeared, miners had discovered the weakness of ordinary trade unions facing employers allied with state and federal authorities. And after its founding in 1893 events in Idaho and Colorado illustrated further the weaknesses inherent in a "pure and simple" trade union. Weakness drove the Western miners toward radicalism, and radicalism apparently resulted in strength and success.

Twice in the Coeur d'Alenes, in 1892 and 1899, miners' unions were impotent against concentrated capital and hostile state and federal forces. Although miners at first elicited sympathy and support from the local middle class, controlled municipal and county offices, and published the community's leading newspapers, their local power proved insufficient. Mine owners, organized in an employers' association, influenced the Governor, maintained their own newspaper just across the state line in Spokane, and kept their own judge in the Idaho federal district court to hand down sweeping injunctions. When injunctions failed to end strikes and state militia proved inadequate and unwilling to repress strikers, Idaho's chief executives, responding to mine owners' pleas, requested federal troops. The reaction of mine owners and state officials was frightening in its implications. Idaho's Attorney-General, for example, demanded of his state's congressional delegation: "The mob must be crushed by overwhelming force"; and to implement his objective, he suggested the use of Gatling guns and howitzers. The Governor and other state officials, counselled by the Mine Owners' Association, demanded the permanent presence of federal troops in northern Idaho to prevent future troubles and protect citizens against guerrilla warfare.

Idaho's mine owners and state officials did not desist until they had crushed the miners' unions. In 1899, again abetted by federal troops, they incarcerated workers and strike sympathizers in the infamous bullpen and denied employment to union miners. Some of those who had defended the self-same miners in 1892 now turned against them. James H. Hawley, together with his junior associate, William Borah, prosecuted the union leaders he had defended in court seven years earlier. His one-time warm political friends had become dangerous criminals. Hawley also engaged in the extracurricular practice of organizing a company union. "No matter how it [the court case] goes," he wrote to his law partner, "we will win our fight by breaking the power of the Union." The corporations had finally succeeded in polarizing Idaho politics and society. Against this type of activity, the W.F.M. and particularly President Boyce, a former Coeur d'Alene miner, found strict trade union tactics unavailing.

The W.F.M. learned the same bitter lesson in Colorado. With the aid of a Populist Governor, "Bloody Bridles" Waite, they had defeated a mine owners' private army in 1894. But two years later with a Republican in the State House, mine owners obtained the state militia to break a strike in Leadville. After the unsuccessful Leadville strike of 1896, the W.F.M. made the crucial shift to the left in politics and practice.

As the union moved further left, Colorado's Mine Owners' Association prepared to turn to its own advantage American fear of radicalism and socialism. In 1902 mine owners formed a state-wide organization to combat unions with money, propaganda, and Pinkertons. Simultaneously they enlisted the aid of local businessmen and professionals previously allied with the miners. Again the process of social polarization came relatively late and was consummated on the initiative of the larger corporate interests. By February 24, 1903, Boyce's successor as president of the W.F.M., Charles Moyer, informed union members: "We are being attacked on all sides at this time by the Mill Trust and Mine Owners' Association."

W.F.M. officials, although on the defensive, tried to negotiate with Colorado employers. During a dispute with Colorado City mill and smelter operators, Moyer emphasized that the purpose of the W.F.M. was to build, not destroy—to avoid by all honorable means a war between employer and employee. But Haywood, at the same time, probably described the W.F.M.'s position more accurately: ". . . We are not opposed to employers, and it is our purpose and aim to work harmoniously and jointly with the employers as best we can under this system, and we intend to change the system if we get sufficiently organized and well enough educated to do so." In brief, union leaders separated long-term from immediate goals: in the short-run they barely differed from the AFL, but the America they desired for the future was vastly different from and hardly acceptable to the AFL or to the American business community.

Corporate interests in Colorado, like corporations elsewhere in America, would have no compromise with labor for the short run or the long run. Company attorneys callously viewed labor as another commodity to be bought and sold in the market place; and company managers denied to unions, the state, and the public the right to intervene in company affairs. Between management's deepest commitments and W.F.M. objectives, compromise was impossible; thus a delicately balanced *modus vivendi* collapsed and a miniature civil war erupted in Colorado's Cripple Creek district in 1903-04.

The W.F.M.'s now clear desire to abolish the prevailing economic system turned previously moderate employers against the union. Employers *might* tolerate and bargain with a labor organization prepared to accept the *status quo,* but not one dedicated to the abolition of capitalism. Nation-wide corporations, local businessmen, and state and national officials united to rid the West of working-class radicalism. Martial law gripped Colorado's mining districts. Military officers made, administered, and executed the law, flaunting with impunity established courts. The W.F.M. Executive Board declared a state of open war in Colorado in December 1903 but still maintained its willingness to compromise: "The

W.F. of M. has at all times been ready and willing to go more than half way in meeting the Mine Operators of the State, and use every honorable means to bring a close to this conflict, that has left scars upon the welfare and prosperity of every citizen of the State." Though the W.F.M. preferred negotiation, employers, aware of their unity and strength, crushed the union in Colorado.

☆　　☆　　☆

Industrial conflicts in the Coeur d'Alenes, Leadville, and Cripple Creek convinced W.F.M. leaders of the need to convert their organization from an industrial union concerned with wages and jobs, into an advocate of revolutionary change and socialism. The W.F.M. had been formed after the first Coeur d'Alene conflict. After the 1896 Leadville debacle, Boyce castigated Gompers and the AFL, called upon union miners to join rifle clubs, and demanded a more radical brand of politics. Then, as both Democrats and Republicans turned against labor and allied with corporate interests while middle-class friends deserted it, the W.F.M. became more radical as well as more politically conscious. The organization's adoption of Marxian Socialism (1900-03) finally completed the process of social polarization in the urban-industrial centers of the Mountain West as the W.F.M. lost the remainder of its local middle-class allies. Simultaneously, for the same reasons, the Western labor organizations came into overt conflict with Gompers and the AFL.

Western hostility to Gompers was of long standing, as he had not been forgiven for destroying the Knights of Labor and neglecting the Populists. As early as 1894, when John McBride defeated Gompers for the AFL presidency, the Western Federation's official paper exulted: ". . . good riddance of bad rubbish," and later it accused Gompers of belonging "to that class of leaders which is fast being relegated to the rear—a narrow-minded, self-seeking, and trouble breeding element." During the 1896 Leadville conflict, when AFL assistance to striking miners proved negligible, Boyce and Gompers debated the deficiencies of the AFL and the advantages of radical unionism. Gompers warned Boyce against breaking with the AFL and bringing grief to the house of labor, while Boyce informed the AFL leader that Western workers were 100 years ahead of their Eastern comrades. Thus the W.F.M. at its 1897 convention withdrew from the AFL, to which it had belonged for only a year, and established a rival regional labor organization.

The W.F.M.'s Executive Board in 1898, following similar attempts by Montana's State Trades and Labor Council, invited all Western unions to attend a meeting in Salt Lake City to organize the Western Labor Union. A loyal AFL man described the new Western labor organization to Gompers as ". . . only the Western Federation of Miners under another name. . . . Boyce dominated everything. . . . Boyce's influence with the miners is unquestionably strong. The majority believe him sincerely, and all of them fear to oppose him."

Western workers, during the Salt Lake meeting, stressed their desire to escape conservative unionism and demanded an industrial, educational, and political organization, uncompromising in policy and ". . . broad enough in principle and sufficiently humane in character to embrace every class of toil, from the farmer to the skilled mechanic, in one great brotherhood." The new Western Labor Union insisted that industrial technology had made trade-union methods obsolete and left the working class but one recourse: ". . . to take up the arms of a modern revolutionary period . . . the free and intelligent use of the ballot." Thus in 1900 the W.L.U.'s newspaper endorsed the socialist ticket, and its 1901 convention adopted a preamble and platform denouncing American government, "the very foundations of which is crumbling to decay, through the corruption and infamy of the self-constituted governing class. . . ." The W.L.U. professed to be ready to spill every drop of its blood at the point of a bayonet rather than submit to further capitalistic aggressions. If the W.L.U. intended to frighten conservative America, it succeeded.

The differences between the AFL and Western labor grew. Even those W.F.M. members who favored union with the AFL did so as Western missionaries, not as true believers in Gompersism; they insisted that in the face of united capital, labor must do likewise or fail. "We must try to teach our benighted brothers in the 'jungles of New York' and [in] the East what we have learned here in the progressive, enterprising West."[2] This attitude, which represented the more conservative elements of the W.F.M., could lead only to conflict. Suddenly AFL organizers appeared in the previously neglected Mountain States to compete with their W.L.U. counterparts. In Denver, AFL organizers tried to destroy W.L.U. locals. Insisting that it had only attempted to organize the unorganized within its territory, the W.L.U., through its Executive Board, informed the AFL that it was too busy battling corporations to seek a fight with another labor organization. "If the officers and members of organized labor will do their duty, the Western Federation of Miners, the

[2] Of course, I must agree with Perlman and Taft that local conditions had something to do with Western dualism, but to concentrate on geographical peculiarities is to overlook what were real ideological differences. Western workers, as shown above, had radical backgrounds. They had engaged in partisan political activity and would continue to do so, and they supported industrial unionism of a strong social reformist nature. While Western short-run objectives—higher wages, reduced hours, etc.—did not differ basically from those of AFL unions, their long-run aims and their avowed opposition to time contracts flaunted basic AFL principles.

Western Labor Union included, there is a broad field for all while ninety per cent of those who toil remain unorganized."

Instead of submitting to the AFL's demands, Western workers became more aggressive. They carefully catalogued the indignities which the W.F.M. had borne with extreme patience, but warned: ". . . there comes a time in the history of all such imposition when patience ceases to be a virtue, and this juncture for the Western Federation of Miners has now arrived." In the spring of 1902, when the AFL sent two delegates to the W.F.M. convention urging re-affiliation with the Federation, the W.F.M.'s journal commented: "The Western Federation of Miners and the Western Labor Union are ready to join forces with any labor organization that offers a remedy, but they don't propose to be led like sheep into a slaughter pen to await the butcher's knife without a struggle." Thus the W.F.M., instead of dissolving the W.L.U. and returning to Gompers' waiting arms, transformed the W.L.U. into the American Labor Union and more firmly embraced socialism.

The American Labor Union, considered by Paul Brissenden the climactic development in the evolution of industrial unionism of the political-socialist type, appeared too radical and too revolutionary for some socialists. While party leaders welcomed the A.L.U.'s endorsement, they deprecated its war upon the AFL, compared the A.L.U. to DeLeon's infamous Socialist Trades and Labor Alliance, and refused to acknowledge its existence as a recognized national labor organization. The socialist left, however, immediately rose to defend the Westerners. Debs characterized Western labor as militant, progressive, liberal in spirit, with a class-conscious political program. "The class-conscious movement of the West," he wrote, "is historic in origin and development and every Socialist should recognize its mission and encourage its growth. It is here that the tide of social revolution will reach its flood and thence roll into other sections, giving impetus where needed and hastening the glorious day of triumph."

Clearly little room for compromise existed between Western radicals and Eastern labor leaders. The AFL could not allow its Western competitor to enter national organizing territory without suffering potential losses. By the same token, the A.L.U., a declared enemy of capitalism, could not inch closer to the AFL, whose leader it accused of being controlled absolutely by capitalism. Instead the Western radicals defied Gompers, continued to organize the unorganized of the West, and made threatening gestures east of the Mississippi and even of the Hudson. "We believe that the time has arrived when our organization should say in no uncertain language to this band of disruptionists [AFL leaders], 'hands off'," the W.F.M.'s Executive Board announced at the end of 1902. "We have no desire to interfere with their organization and demand that they discontinue their efforts to create disruption in our ranks."

The more radical the W.F.M. became, the more it grew, and the more popular its president became among Western workers. By 1900 the W.F.M. had won the warm backing of Debs, who became more enthusiastic as the Western organization heightened its political consciousness and radicalism. In January 1902, Debs, accepting an invitation to address the coming convention, responded: "I have always felt that your organization is the most radical and progressive national body in the country, and I have it in my mind that it is to take a commanding part, if it does not lead, in the social revolution that will insure final emancipation to the struggling masses." The 1902 convention made Debs still happier by formally endorsing socialism, founding the American Labor Union and proclaiming, in Boyce's farewell address, "Trade unions have had a fair trial, and it has been clearly demonstrated that they are unable to protect their members."

While union leaders were most responsible for converting the W.F.M. into a socialist organization, the rank and file exhibited no strong reservations about such radicalism, for in a labor organization more democratic than most, ideologically equivocal officials would have been removed. When Boyce retired, his successor, Charles Moyer, was equally committed to socialism. Moyer immediately reaffirmed the W.F.M.'s commitment to independent political action in "a determined effort to bring about such a change in our social and economic conditions as will result in a complete revolution of the present system of industrial slavery." He found politics and socialism no bar to union growth and in fact claimed that radicalism was responsible for growth in the number of locals and members. Correspondence to the W.F.M.'s journal from rank and filers also showed a heavy preponderance in favor of independent political action and socialism.[3] While the political views of the majority of W.F.M. mem-

---

[3] While there is apparently no way to quantify, the political sentiments of W.F.M. members and thus dispute exists as to the extent of radicalism and socialism in the union, the available evidence suggests strong socialist leanings. The mining-smelter areas, especially Butte and Denver, were the strongest socialist regions in the Mountain West and among the strongest in the nation. The letters-to-the-editor column of the *Miners Magazine* was open to all variety of opinions, even those opposed to official WFM policy, but the bulk of the letters from rank and filers and local unions endorsed either socialism or other forms of independent political action. The testimony of labor leaders and rank-and-file hard-rock miners before a government commission showed overt hostility to capitalism and explicit endorsement of public ownership of the basic means of production. As late as 1906, W.F.M. rank and filers refused to co-operate with the AFL's political programme because it was based on employer-employee harmony.

bers are unclear, a significant, literate, and articulate union group certainly evinced an abiding concern for a radical transformation of American society.

☆   ☆   ☆

Politics and socialism, however, did not by themselves bring the new dawn. Local battles were won but the employers allied with the older parties controlling state and national governments seemed to be winning the war. "Pure and simple" trade unionism may have failed but seemingly so had socialism. Consequently, just as Populism gave way to socialism and the W.L.U. to the A.L.U., socialism was to give way to syndicalism and the A.L.U. to the I.W.W.

The W.F.M. in 1904, admitting the failure of its two previous attempts at dual unionism, tried for a third time with the Industrial Workers of the World. Much in the same way that the W.L.U. and the A.L.U. had been the Western Federation in disguise, the I.W.W. for two years was simply the Western Federation plus a smattering of fellow-travelers. Though W.F.M. and I.W.W. broke sharply in 1907, the Western Federation could not fully deny its progeny. To an earlier generation of less sophisticated, more provincial Americans, Wobblies appeared the greatest threat to the established order—in short, "a clear and present danger."

The foundation of the Industrial Workers of the World seemed to confirm a prophecy made by Friedrich Engels in 1893. "In America, at least," he wrote, "I am strongly inclined to believe that the fatal hour of capitalism will have struck as soon as a native American working class will have replaced a working class composed in its majority by foreign immigrants." The men who created the I.W.W. were by and large native Americans, or the most Americanized immigrants, committed to interring capitalism in America. In a sense, as Engels prophesied, the most radical working-class movement in American history, the one most feared by capitalists and government officials, came not from alien radicals but from native revolutionaries. And today it remains well worth asking, why?

Though no simple and complete answers are at hand, some facts are apparent. The American West, through an unique conjunction of circumstances produced the conditions most conducive to radical unionism. This region's industrialism altered social and economic arrangements more rapidly and drastically than elsewhere in America. Modern technology and corporate capitalism advanced too quickly for smooth adjustment; the rapid pace of economic growth resulted in individual failures and frustrations, social breakdowns, and mob violence. Seeking to stabilize competition, rationalize work processes, and reduce costs, Western corporations encountered a labor force less tractable than the uprooted and ethnically-divided immigrants of the East. The American West, like early industrial England, produced militant and destructive working-class demonstrations. Mining corporations and smelting companies could only control and discipline their workers with assistance from state and federal authorities. The alliance between corporate capitalism and government, which succeeded in polarizing Western society, convinced Western workers that the American nation suffered from grave political and social disorders which could be cured only through revolutionary action. Their past, their experiences, and their hopes for the future shaped Western miners into radicals and revolutionaries.

In a larger sense, however, the development of radical unionism and the emergence of syndicalism in the American West was hardly unique. Simultaneously, thousands of miles removed geographically and farther away socially and spiritually, Italian and French labor organizations declared for syndicalism. The origins of radical unionism in America, France, or Italy thus must be sought in the process of capitalist growth and the larger trends transforming the industrial world. Today we need fewer vague generalizations about the uniqueness or significance of the American frontier and more intensive studies of social and economic structures in the capitalist, industrial, and urban American West. We also need comparative studies placing American labor history in the broader context of world-wide economic history, where all workers, regardless of nationality, tasted the fruits, both bitter and sweet, of the capitalist order.

Voluntarism:
The Political Functions of
an Anti-Political Doctrine

MICHAEL ROGIN

A distinctive ideology—voluntarism—accompanied the trade-union emphasis on immediate, limited goals to be won through the application of economic power. Samuel Gompers, its principal architect, intended the doctrine of voluntarism to serve two purposes: first, to justify collective action by workingmen in an era of rampant individualism, and second, to draw a sharp line setting trade unionism apart from the political sector. In this sophisticated essay, Michael Rogin takes a second look at voluntarism. Locating its intellectual sources in "the revolt against formalism" of the late nineteenth century, Rogin discovers that voluntarism itself ironically turned into a rigid, abstract doctrine. Contrary to Selig Perlman's thesis, American trade unionism proved not immune to dogmatism, even in the absence of middle-class intellectuals. Influenced by Philip Selznick and Grant McConnell in their studies of the TVA and the American Farm Bureau Federation, Rogin argues that voluntarism, while claiming to serve the entire American working class, in fact operated exclusively on behalf of an entrenched trade-union leadership and its narrow craft constituency. The rigid rules of trade autonomy (which defined the internal order of the movement) and antistatism (which defined its relations with the larger society) both rested on the doctrine of voluntarism and both sustained the American Federation of Labor as a haven for an aristocracy of labor. Persuasive as intellectual history, Rogin's analysis needs to be placed in the institutional context in which voluntarism became the doctrinal justification for the labor *status quo*. Doubtless such a study would moderate Rogin's harsh conclusions.

From Michael Rogin, "Voluntarism: The Political Functions of an Anti-Political Doctrine," *The Industrial and Labor Relations Review*, XV (July, 1962), pp. 521–535. Reprinted by permission of the publisher. Footnotes have been omitted except where they amplify the text.

PERHAPS THE MOST COMMON STATEMENT MADE ABOUT THE AMERican labor movement is that it is essentially pragmatic. This observation usually refers to its nonideological character in contrast with the "doctrinaire Marxism" of European unions. When Sam Gompers spoke of the "pragmatism" of the American Federation of Labor, however, he referred to American labor's rejection, not only of European socialism, but also of American Social Darwinism as well. Social Darwinism, which provided the operative ideals for many post-Civil War Americans, was optimistic about individual capacity for economic achievement and fatalistic about political or collective action to change economic conditions. In the name of individual freedom and immutable natural laws, Social Darwinists opposed union organization. Social Darwinist doctrines were generally accepted in the America of the period. They were particularly useful for businessmen anxious to block the growth of unions.

Gompers opposed the doctrines of Social Darwinism as meaningless abstractions, contradicted by the concrete experience of American workers. Laboring men had learned that the Horatio Alger dream was for most of them only a dream, and that they could only improve their situation collectively. In contrast to the Social Darwinist advice to workers, the AFL stressed the benefits of voluntary collective action and labor unity. Yet even as this AFL outlook became articulated, the Federation adopted many Social Darwinist texts. Eventually voluntarism, as the Federation called its "pragmatic" philosophy, conflicted with the needs of the workers and with the growth of the AFL. This happened because voluntarism became, not the practical expression of American working class experience, but an organizational ideology protecting the craft union officials of the AFL.[1]

In its original conception, the unifying theme of voluntarism was that workers could best achieve their goals by relying on their own voluntary associations. Voluntarism defended the autonomy of the international craft union against the coercive interference of the state, the AFL itself and, implicitly, the union membership. Concretely this meant that Federation spokesmen favored trade union autonomy from the Federation and opposed internal union factions. Moreover, it meant opposition to alliance with any political party, as well as to positive state action such as wage-and-hour laws and unemployment insurance.

It would be a mistake to treat voluntarism, the doctrine of an organization, as a coherent and systematic political theory. Gompers and other

---

[1] The idea that ideologies which allegedly come from the grass roots in fact serve organizational purposes is developed by Philip Selznick in *T.V.A. and the Grass Roots* (Berkeley, Calif.: University of California Press, 1949).

AFL spokesmen defended voluntarism with practical arguments. They argued that the AFL could best achieve its goals within the organization by relying on the voluntary cooperation of the internationals. In their attack on politics, they pointed to the difficulty of getting workers to agree on political programs. They stressed the obstacles to the passage of favorable legislation. Perhaps the main emphasis was on the role of courts in emasculating labor legislation and in issuing labor injunctions.

Increasingly as the AFL matured, however, voluntarism was also defended with abstract and theoretical arguments. These arguments, reminiscent of the rhetoric of the Social Darwinist employers against whom the unions had organized, stressed the benefits of an abstract freedom at the expense of more immediate considerations. Opposing unemployment insurance at the 1930 convention, delegate Olander said,

> Every system of unemployment insurance here contemplates supervision and control by both federal and state governments and will require registration, not only of aliens among the workers, but of all of us. . . . Have we lost courage to the point where we regard freedom as no longer the greatest essential of life and the most necessary element in human progress?

At the same time that the AFL used such theoretical arguments to justify craft-union autonomy and to attack state action, it asserted that voluntarism was a "pragmatic philosophy." Voluntarism, it was claimed, was practical and functional, adapting policies to meet the emergent needs of the labor movement. Traditionally, labor historians have not analyzed voluntarism as an organizational ideology, but have accepted its pragmatic claims at face value, ignoring the AFL's theoretical defence of voluntarism. The traditional view has been that voluntarism was the most effective response of American workers to their concrete needs, that it was modified in practice, and that Gompers was a realist who "would not have hesitated to abandon voluntarism had he been convinced that another philosophy would produce more lasting results."

In his *Theory of the Labor Movement,* Selig Perlman provided the theoretical basis for this view of the AFL, where he explained its attitudes, particularly its concentration on job control and economic matters, on the basis of the "manualist consciousness" of the workers. To this consciousness of "organic labor," Perlman, like Gompers, contrasted the antipragmatic, abstract, and philosophical conceptions of intellectuals.

The pragmatic element in voluntarism was real enough, but not the only element. Certainly the AFL was non-revolutionary, and pragmatic in that sense. But pragmatic has other meanings. When Perlman and Gompers called voluntarism pragmatic, they meant that it was useful for the generality of American workers and arose from their actual experience. Once the organization enters the analysis, however, this general pragmatism can no longer be assumed. Voluntarism was indeed practical and protective for a particular small constituency, but it was merely formalist and doctrinaire for the larger constituency for which the American Federation of Labor claimed to speak. In fact, voluntarism was an abstract philosophy, which neither arose nor maintained itself simply out of organized labor's unfavorable experience with the state. In the service of the organization, voluntarism became as doctrinaire and abstract as the Social Darwinism which it opposed.

ORGANIZED LABOR AND
THE PRAGMATIST REVOLT

If voluntarism is to be treated as an organizational ideology, the early AFL must first be understood in the context of the developing social thought of its time. Generally, throughout the nineteenth century the American labor movement had been part of the general reform movements in the nation. The Knights of Labor had been concerned with virtually the whole range of problems agitating American society. The American Federation of Labor, largely neglecting these broad concerns, was a new departure in American labor.[2]

The craft unions' decision to unite workers on the narrow basis of common craft interest has been rightly attributed by Perlman to the difficulty of maintaining an organized labor movement. But, unlike their predecessors, the AFL craft workers strove to create homogeneous unions so that the diverse interests of American workers would not tear the unions apart. As an organization built on this narrow class-constituency of craft workers, the AFL's ideology was meant to protect only the interests of this constituency. But heir to a labor tradition which spoke not only for all workers but for all common men, it attempted to present itself as the spokesman for all American workers. Much of its legitimacy came from its claim to represent this broad constituency, and the organizational ideology had to perpetuate that claim. To identify the voluntarism of the AFL with the pragmatism of its time, however, obscures the fact that what

[2] For a similar departure in agricultural politics, see Grant McConnell, *The Decline of Agrarian Democracy* (Berkeley, Calif., The University of California Press, 1953). I treat the AFL as attempting to create a homogeneous organization through building itself up on a narrow craft worker constituency, yet claiming to speak for the board constituency of the working class. This approach was suggested by McConnell's treatment of the Farm Bureau.

is functional for one group may be dysfunctional for others, and ignores the differentiated groups within the American working class.

As the ideology of the American Federation of Labor, voluntarism was subject to currents which influenced other American thought. The founders of the AFL, discontented with the status quo, shared the outlook of American social thinkers at the turn of the century. Here was the same devotion to concrete reality, the same attack on abstract, formal and metaphysical approaches found in Dewey, Robinson, Holmes, Beard, and others. Morton White, in his *Social Thought in America,* has called attention to the antiformalist character of American social thought in this period.[3] In challenging the conservatism of the late nineteenth century, the new trade unions thus joined the revolt against formalism. When questioned by the Socialist, Morris Hillquit, Gompers acknowledged that the various spheres of social life were interrelated and vigorously denied that the AFL restricted its activity to any one field. Asked whether it had a general social philosophy, Gompers replied,

> It is guided by the history of the past, drawing its lessons from history. It knows the conditions by which working people are surrounded. It works along the line of least resistance and endeavors to accomplish the best results in improving the conditions of the working people, men, women, and children, today and tomorrow. . . .

A claim to realism, based on "historicism" and "cultural organicism," was also the main positive element in the thinkers about whom White writes. Moreover, the similarities between their antiformalism and that of the AFL were not confined to generalities. For example, the legal theory of the revolt against formalism stressed the historical development of the law and rejected the view that the law evolved in accordance with a formal-logical pattern. Legal formalism was used against the trade union, so that Gompers wrote:

> The change that labor aims to effect in the courts is to infuse into legalism ideals, interpretations, and a conscience that are social. Professor Roscoe Pound defines the social formula of justice as an attempt to secure individual interests because, and to the extent that, they are social.

The antiformalist theory of law recognized the social transformation that was taking place in America. All the writers stressed the primarily economic character of this transformation. Recognizing the limitations

---

[3] By formalism is meant, here and throughout, abstract ideas which particular groups claim to be in the general interest but actually use to attack action against their own interests.

on freedom caused by the new economic power, Dewey distinguished between real and formal freedom. Formal freedom was a condition for effective freedom, but there were other conditions, such as the power to achieve one's goal.

By its very existence, of course, the AFL attested to the importance of economic liberty. The antiformalist distinction between real and formal freedom was thus crucial to an organization whose purpose was to fight for real freedom against a dogmatism of formal freedom. In a speech in Chicago in 1908, Gompers said:

> Rights? Yes, there is no hesitancy on the part of our courts to grant us certain rights—for instance, the rights to be maimed or killed without any responsibility to the employer; the right to be discharged for belonging to a union of labor; the right to work as long hours for as low wages as the employer can impose upon working men or women. These rights—these academic rights which we do not want—are frequently conceded, but there is a denial to us of the rights that are essential to our welfare.

This distinction between essential and academic rights, real and formal freedom, is related to the recognition that, as Gompers put it:

> We are not in an ideal world. . . . We are in the bitter struggles of an unjust society. . . . To shift applications of axioms that spring from the principles of abstract liberty to a totally different set of axioms that arise from manifest injustices of a present society—that is the mental juggle of dishonest liberty and property defense leaguers.

John Dewey expressed this thought in a sentence. "No ends are accomplished without the use of force." It would seem that Gompers could accept this formulation. Thus he wrote,

> In a hundred different directions the freedom of the citizen in modern society is restricted in the interests of the general welfare, or of public good, or health and morals. . . .
> Professor Seligman's very acute analysis of economic liberty clearly exhibits the truth that we can never enjoy liberty in any absolute sense, that "all social progress is a result of certain repression of the liberty of some in the interests of all."

If this were the only side of Gompers' attitude toward coercion, there would be no ambivalence in the pragmatism of the AFL or in its relation to the revolt against formalism. Voluntarism, however, rejected the antiformalist acceptance of force and opposed all restrictions on liberty. In his last speech to the AFL, Gompers said, "I want to urge devotion to the fundamentals of human liberty—the principles of voluntarism. No lasting gain has ever come from coercion." It is this principled attack on force that differentiated voluntarism from the revolt against formalism. But if voluntarism is to be treated as a theory, its departure from the pragmatism of the period must be explained.

INDIVIDUALISM AND THE
PROBLEM OF COERCION

The most obvious revolt of the trade union was against the formalism of individualism.

> To say that a working man loses his individualism or his sovereignty in joining a union of labor is begging the question entirely. The fact of the matter is as soon as a man enters an industrial plant he loses his individuality and becomes a cog in a great revolving machine.
> It is by sacrificing his theoretical freedom of contract as an individual and by merging himself in an association with his fellows that the wage earner in many trades finally secures improved conditions of living.

The attack on abstract individualism—expressed concretely in the organization of unions—was the essence of the AFL's revolt against formalism. But the creation of groups led to an abstract "group individualism" which destroyed that revolt. Laboring men, revolting against a conservative formalism which had protected the interests of the business classes, had built new organizations. But these new organizations had to be legitimized to members, to the public, and had to be protected against attack from without and within. The main function of the ideology of voluntarism was to protect these organizations.

The American Federation of Labor had implicitly taken a formalist text from Rousseau. "The problem," Rousseau had written, "is to find a form of association . . . in which each, while uniting himself with all, may still remain as free as before." According to Dewey, in joining unions workers sacrificed a largely meaningless freedom for a meaningful freedom. But the arguments the Federation presented to defend the closed shop, the boycott, and other union activities indicated that, where union activity and organization were concerned, it departed from Dewey's realistic position. Coercion, it was argued, ceased to be always present and always necessary, and disappeared both from within the union and from a totally organized economy.

In defending union activities, Gompers used the word "freedom" in the same formalist sense that he bitterly attacked when it was used against the trade union. Attempting to legitimize the union against the Spencerian attacks, he accepted the absolutist judicial notions current at the time, and used them to defend the trade union. Thus, in opposing the injunction, the Federation cited the constitutional guarantees of the first amendment. But it cited them as absolute prerogatives, which under no circumstances might be abridged. This "absolute-rights" theory was not supported by the legal realists. Holmes wrote, "No conduct has such absolute privilege as to justify all possible schemes of which it may be a part." Defending the closed shop Gompers wrote,

> Organized workmen have the right to refuse to work with unorganized workmen. Such a refusal is an exercise of their own right of contract and it cannot therefore be a violation of the right of anyone else. . . . The employers are free—free in a legal or moral sense of course—to choose between the organized and the unorganized. If he [sic] prefers the former for economic reasons, because they are more efficient or productive, the latter have no grievance either against him or against the workmen chosen.

It had been the argument of Brandeis and of the trade union, that the whole problem of coercion existed in the economy because the exercise of one party's "right of contract" was likely to be a violation of someone else's rights in a world of unequal power. This insight had undermined the classical conception of a free and spontaneous (that is, unregulated) economy. But what Gompers sought to do was simply to raise spontaneous economic action to a higher level. An economy of organized groups would operate without coercion and could, therefore, be unregulated.[4] Politics (that is, the exercise of power) had become necessary because of the existence of and need for groups, but Gompers affirmed "that right is not made wrong, nor wrong right, by mere numbers. What a thousand men may do individually, they may do as a combination." In so defending the boycott, Gompers failed to recognize that the difference between one worker acting and a thousand workers acting as one is that the thousand have more power. Gompers justified their acting by implying that unions were not exercising power; the proper justification is that other power already exists in the society. By defending the abstract, formal freedom to boycott, Gompers ignored the coercive power exercised by boycotting unions. He was thus able to preserve the fiction that coercion was absent in an economy of competing groups. If coercion were absent, state action in the economy would simply substitute force for freedom.

[4] In his autobiography Gompers wrote, "I have often allowed myself to dream of the possibilities of production if all were free to work unretarded by the existing restraints. . . . Foremost in my mind is to tell the politicians to keep their hands off and thus preserve voluntary institutions and opportunities for individual and group initiative. . . ." Except for the inclusion of groups, this reproduces the views of Social Darwinists and businessmen of the late nineteenth century.

In the arguments it used to defend trade union activities, regardless of their effects, the AFL departed from the main revolt against formalism. Because its defenses of trade union action were philosophic and formalistic, however, it hardly follows that these defenses were impractical. The antithesis of pragmatism in that sense and formalism simply obscure the real issue. In fact, the formalism of the AFL was meant to be useful, but it was useful for the organization.[5]

THE INTERNAL USES OF VOLUNTARISM

If voluntarism departed from the revolt against formalism because it was an organizational ideology, then it becomes important to understand the organizational interests it served. Voluntarism served functions for the union leaders analogous to the functions served for radicals by Leninism. Both theories subordinated the organizations to the goals of a particular constituency. Thus, within the AFL, voluntarism legitimized the power of the large craft union internationals, and it legitimized the power of the leadership both within the Federation and within the internationals themselves.

Applying the principles of voluntary action to support the freedom of the international unions, the Federation denied to itself the right to intervene in the affairs of its affiliates. Thereby, voluntarism ignored the problems of coercion that existed within the internationals. Many commentators have argued that the Federation was too weak to interfere with its affiliates. Indeed, the policy of non-intervention was based on a recognition of power realities, but according to voluntarism, the policy was directed to the goal of freedom. By converting a power reality into a moral attitude, the Federation implicitly denied that power was a problem at all within the unions. By denying that an unequal distribution of power existed, voluntarism helped perpetuate the existing distribution. An ideology which attacked force was used to justify an existing distribution of force.

Voluntarism not only avoided the problem of internal government, it also contributed more directly to the support of craft union officialdom. In its attack on force, voluntarism expressed the ideal of an organization without internal conflict. Implicitly, force was unnecessary because the unions were homogeneous institutions making up a homogeneous federa-

---

[5] At no point in the argument do I mean to imply that the advocacy of voluntarism by the leaders of the AFL was insincere. The argument that voluntarism served organizational functions does not go to the question of whether its proponents were "really" motivated by self-interest, organizational interest, concern for the membership, or concern for the whole working class.

tion in which agreement on ends could be achieved voluntarily. Gompers' farewell speech makes it clear that the ideal of unanimity is associated with an absolute denial of coercion.

> I want to urge devotion to the fundamentals of human liberty—the principles of voluntarism. No lasting gain has ever come from compulsion. If we seek to force we but tear apart that which, united, is invincible. There is no way whereby our labor movement may be assured sustained progress in determining its policies and plans other than sincere democratic deliberation until a unanimous decision is reached.

Of course, there was unanimity on few issues in the Federation and compromise, or the imposition of the view of the most powerful, was the actual practice. But by arguing that Federation decisions had unanimous approval (since they adhered to the principles of voluntarism), Gompers made it appear that there were no dissident points of view and no unequal distribution of power behind the expressed decisions of the Federation. He thereby attempted to legitimize the AFL externally as the spokesman for "labor," and internally against potential membership revolts.

Moreover, since unions were homogeneous, internal organization of differing points of view was unnecessary. Thus Gompers attacked a socialist faction in his own cigar-makers' union.

> We must ourselves permit of the free and untrammelled expression of opinion by the members of an organization, and not by a clique formed within the organization to control the business, the legislation, and the election of officers who are to control the affairs of the organization.

The belief in homogeneity of interests, and the resulting attack on factions, served to make the group a concrete reality. By ignoring the problems of differential power in the economy, voluntarism had given the group an appearance of external reality and promoted a theory of group individualism. Similarly, voluntarism ignored the problem of union government. Oblivious to different points of view within the Federation, voluntarism legitimized the most powerful view, that of craft union officialdom. Ignoring the conflict between leaders and members, voluntarism legitimized the leaders as the spokesmen for the group. And if the leadership was the legitimate group spokesman, then those criticizing the leaders became attackers of the union.

Voluntarism, in fact, is a theory of democracy which emerges from the homogeneity of a small group. It finds clear expression in Rousseau.

> But when factions arise, and partial associations are formed at the expense of the great association, the will of each of these associations

becomes general in relation to its members, while it remains particular in relation to the state. . . . It is therefore essential, if the general will is to be able to express itself, that there should be no partial society within the state. . . .

When this theory of democracy is applied within a large and diverse society, as it was in the nineteenth-century French liberals' attack on parties and in Gompers' attack on factions, it helps to perpetuate oligarchy. Operationally, the leaders represent the general will of the group. In the absence of organized centers for opposition to the current "general will," changing it, or changing those who represent it, becomes difficult.

Thus voluntarism, by ignoring the problem of power in the name of an abstract defense of freedom, legitimized the existing power distribution and attacked the legitimacy of attempts to change it. And if the power of craft union officialdom was behind the Federation's defense of trade autonomy, this same power led it to take positive action to support the large craft unions and their leaders.

Thus, despite the theory of voluntarism, the Federation interfered with the trade autonomy of the small internationals at the behest of the larger ones. The 1899 resolution on trade autonomy adopted by the AFL convention declared that the Federation was founded on the principle of the absolute self-government of all the crafts and guaranteed the weaker crafts the same protection as the stronger. This was the theory, but it was not the organizational reality. In jurisdictional disputes between large and small crafts, not only did the Federation often use the theory of voluntarism to refuse to intervene to help the smaller crafts, but it also often intervened to help the larger craft unions. The Mule Spinners, for example, argued that to be forced by the Federation to amalgamate with the Textile Workers violated their trade autonomy. This argument, theoretically impeccable, did not stop their forced amalgamation. Coercion was used against those elements whose antagonism was least likely to hurt the AFL.

In the area of internal union affairs, in spite of its professions of noninterference within the internationals, the Federation sided with the established leadership against rank-and-file revolts. Regardless of the conditions, no factions which had seceded or had been expelled from international unions were recognized. Nor did the Federation ever go so far as to appoint investigating committees. When President Berry of the Printing Pressmen entered the 1923 AFL convention after having suppressed an insurgent strike with some of the most unsavory techniques in labor movement history, he was greeted by Gompers as a savior of the labor movement.

Selig Perlman has contrasted the "vanguard" attitudes resulting from the abstract approach of intellectuals to the working class with the pragmatic manualism of trade union consciousness. It appears from the analysis here that voluntarism concealed a "vanguard" approach to the labor movement by trade union leaders.

THE OPPOSITION TO SOCIAL LEGISLATION

From the early years of the Federation, voluntarism was applied within the Federation in the ways suggested above. In the years before the first World War, however, a socialist opposition kept internal discussion alive and provided a challenge to the leadership. Therefore, during this time, the constraining effects of voluntarism on internal democracy were limited. In the 1920's, there was little or no opposition within the Federation and voluntarism became the unchallenged practice of the organization. And though voluntarism became more dominant within the Federation, its application to internal government did not change. Internally, voluntarism always defended the freedom of trade union leaders.

Externally, however, the meaning of voluntarism changed radically, as the position of the AFL changed in relation to the external world. In the beginning, voluntarism emphasized what the workers could obtain, unaided, through their own organizations. Abstractions which interfered with action and the practical solution of problems were attacked. Describing his early experience Gompers wrote, "My mind intuitively rejected the iron law of wages, the immutable law of supply and demand, and similar so-called natural laws. . . . My unfailing support of voluntary principles reflects my aversion to any theory of economic fatalism."

The AFL's de-emphasis of politics was based on this activist view of what voluntarism meant. "Why wait for the slow process of law," asked Vice-President Duncan, "when we can exert a sure and certain economic power?" Despite such views, the AFL neither emphasized politics nor withdrew completely from political activity. In its very earliest years, the Federation engaged in lobbying and had an extensive political program. From approximately 1899 to 1904, while the AFL was growing rapidly, it became more and more opposed to political activity. Increasing employer and state opposition, however, forced it into a greater emphasis on political action until 1914, when the Clayton Act was passed. Despite this clouded victory, until the New Deal the Federation was to hold the most extreme antistate position in its history.

World War I experience hastened the development of this position. In 1914 the Federation had already opposed eight-hour laws, and antistate

articles began to appear frequently in the *Federationist.* While World War
I brought AFL leaders into participation in government, more significantly,
Federation officials had the experience of participation with management.
To Federation leaders, the war experience taught the value not of govern-
ment action but of union cooperation with industry. Before the war,
Gompers had denied that there was a harmony of interests between labor
and capital. After the war he asserted that this harmony existed.[6] Their
aggravated anxiety to win a place as the partners of industry made the
Federation leaders even more opposed to state interference than they
had been before the war.

At its inception, the AFL had asserted the power of workers to change
their conditions through legislation as well as through union action. It
therefore favored public works, nationalization of the telegraph, and
other positive state action. But as the Federation grew, these positive
proposals were either explicitly repudiated or ignored. Arguing that the
economy must be let alone so that the free institutions within it could
operate without restriction, the Federation opposed wage-and-hour laws
and unemployment insurance. Its main political efforts were directed to
getting the state out of labor affairs, through the removal of such restrictions as the injunction and the application of the antitrust laws to labor.[7]

In the history of the Federation, then, the original meaning of voluntarism became completely altered. At first, voluntarism stressed the power
of free labor unions to obtain their goals. Thirty years later, in the name
of freedom, it denied to unions the right to act politically. Opposing action
in support of social insurance, Gompers explained,

> Sore and sad as I am by the illness, the killing, the maiming of so
> many of my fellow workers, I would rather see that go on for years
> and years, minimized and mitigated by the organized labor movement,
> than give up one jot of the freedom of the workers to strive and struggle
> for their own emancipation through their own efforts.

In the areas of collective bargaining and union organization, the AFL
also became less activist. Federation spokesmen justified their new em-

[6] In 1914 Gompers said, "I say they are not. . . . I know of no means by which
the interests of the employers and the workingmen can be made harmonious in the
full and broad sense of the term." In 1924 he wrote, "Labor, as such, may have
interests that seem to clash with the interests of other factors in industry, but as a
part of the great world of industry, labor, management, science, all share in the
responsibility for the productivity and general well-being of industry. . . ." It is no
accident that this sentiment appeared in an article attacking politicians.

[7] The Federation also favored certain positive legislation, but only to help those
groups that were not perceived as able to help themselves. These groups were
primarily women, children, and federal employees.

phasis on labor-management cooperation with the argument that cooperation was superior to force. The result was dismal organizing campaigns
which tried to convince management rather than the workers of the
virtues of unionism. Voluntarism had come to mean cooperation instead
of self-help. Not self-help but management-help was the alternative to
self-help through politics.

Voluntarism thus changed its meaning as the Federation became an
established organization. In the early period the young organization, heir
to a reform-oriented labor tradition whose legitimacy the AFL hoped to
claim for itself, found it inconvenient to oppose all state action. Moreover,
while the Federation was fighting for an end to the labor injunction
through legislation, it was oriented toward politics, and was more interested
in an alliance with politically minded unionists and reformers than in an
attack on positive state action. While the antistate applications of voluntarism were already visible before 1914, with the passage of the Clayton
Act in that year, which established the AFL's social legitimacy, antistate
voluntarism became dominant.

In the years following the passage of the Clayton Act the most striking
application of antistate voluntarism was the Federation's opposition to
social legislation favored by most other reformers.

Throughout its pre-New Deal history, the AFL opposed unemployment
insurance and minimum-wage laws for men. Though before the turn of
the century it had gone on record in favor of laws regulating hours, in
1914 it "reaffirmed" its opposition to such laws. Here again the difference
between the AFL and the progressive movement of the period requires
explanation.

The basis of AFL opposition to social legislation was the craft union
leader's conception of his union's self-interest. James Duncan, president of
the Stone Cutters and a vice-president of the Federation, made this clear
in the debate on the hours' resolution at the 1914 convention.

> There are many trades working in this Federation whose men are
> working less than eight hours at the present time. In a number of locali-
> ties our trade, looking for a new contract, has it state, "For a shorter
> workday." They have seven and one-half hours and they will get down
> to seven, and we hope through our trade union activities to get down to
> six-hour law by and by. If you have an eight hour law you will see the
> handicap we will have in arguing with our employers for seven and
> seven and one-half hours a day.

This was the antiformalism of a established craft, fearful of the harmful
effects of a law for which, as an organization, it had no need. But it was
precisely the pragmatic argument of Duncan that could not suffice in an

organization which claimed to represent not only the powerful craft unions but also the unorganized workers. What was practical for Duncan was erected in his defense into a formalism that was not practical for the great majority of workers.

Many craft workers did not need to favor wage-and-hour legislation because they could obtain the benefits through their organizations. Here the interests of the class-based craft membership predominated. The unions, however, were powerless to provide other benefits such as unemployment insurance. Here concern for organizational maintenance was crucial. The original attack on the anti-labor character of the existing state was generalized to a fear of any positive state action. Large-scale political action might create institutions such as political parties or autonomous political action committees which would compete with the unions for the workers' loyalties. Large programs of state aid might turn workers' devotion away from the union and toward the state.[8] With these fears, the craft union officials were not willing to expend the resources involved in supporting large-scale political and state action.

Antiunion activities by an antilabor state also contributed to the AFL's opposition to social legislation. But these activities should not obscure the antistate posture deriving from the Federation's position as an established organization. In this respect, the Federation paralleled the laissez-faire capitalists against whom it had organized.

The Federation opposed social legislation for reasons which it perceived as pragmatic. But it was pure formalism, and not pragmatism, to insist that the voluntary association of the workers could be relied upon to provide such benefits as unemployment insurance. In fact, the AFL used ideological arguments to oppose practical reforms to ameliorate the condition of the workers. This is a far cry from pragmatism claimed for it by Gompers and Perlman.

Gompers opposed a New York minimum-wage law for women on the ground that it was "a curb upon the natural rights and opportunity for development of the women of our country and of the industry." In contrast, when the Federation was supporting hours' legislation for women in 1910, John Mitchell had ridiculed a similar argument:

[8] On this last point a statement by John Frey opposing unemployment insurance is revealing. "If you feed lions cooked meat, they are not going to roar. If you want the lions to roar you will have to hold raw meat under their noses, and then they will roar. The only way to get wage-earners interested in the trade union movement and make it a driving force is to convince them that . . . it is only through the strength, the fighting strength of that economic organization that you are going to get higher wages and shorter hours." Frey was one of the two or three most powerful men in the post-Gompers AFL.

The very ground upon which this woman made her complaint—namely that she could not earn enough money in ten hours to maintain herself—renders ridiculous and absurd her plea that her liberty had been abridged.

Gompers also attacked the Socialists for substituting ultimate goals for immediate demands:

The workers have chosen as a policy or pragmatic philosophy . . . immediate and continuous improvement instead of waiting for that far-off period when all the universe shall ring with the rare sweet harmony of perfect accord.

But he also attacked compulsory health insurance:

It is a mere palliative, for economic justice, when established, will bring the relief sought for, and in greater measure, if obtained by the workers through organization, and this can only be done through freedom of action.

Gompers often attacked the Socialists for being concerned with the prevention of evil to the exclusion of amelioration of evil. But in opposing unemployment insurance in 1931, the Executive Council of the Federation explained, "There are just two approaches to this problem: prevention and relief."

This is not the place to recount the struggles in the Federation over social legislation. But this summary of its position and arguments suggests that voluntarism was not simply a pragmatic response of American workers to their situation. Rather it was a formalism which, in the name of abstract ideology, interfered with the workers' practical solutions to their immediate problems. The Federation's abstract notions of natural rights and freedom were pragmatic, not in content but in function, and not in general but for a particular constituency. While in some areas organizational needs corresponded to broad constituency needs, in the area of social legislation the two conflicted.

Moreover, in continuing to adhere to voluntarism after the 1930's depression began, the leadership interfered with organizational interests. True to voluntarism, Federation spokesmen continued their abstract and moral preaching against social legislation and by so doing probably aided the formation of the CIO. Official adherence to the philosophy of voluntarism even into the depression is explainable less by the realism of the Federation's leaders than by their commitment to a rigid philosophy which interfered with practical action in their own interest.

VOLUNTARISM AND LOCAL POLITICS

I have argued that the AFL's opposition to social legislation was perpetuated more by organizational and craft worker concerns than by the antistate feeling of American workers as a whole. This is further supported by an analysis of the role of voluntarism in sustaining local labor political alliances.

Defending Perlman's *Theory*, Philip Taft has written of "its insistence that an understanding of labor and unionism must come from a study of its institutions and practices rather than from theorizing about historical missions." The insistence of the *Theory* that the AFL survived, "mainly because it knew how to resist the lure of politics," and the acceptance of the Federation's claim to nonpartisan politics at face value, however, have led historians largely to ignore the significant local political area of labor's "institutions and practices."

The dominance of the Perlman theory, even among political scientists concerned with the labor movement, has meant that little material is available on the actions of craft unions in city politics. Nevertheless, an examination of the material that is available on New York, Chicago, Philadelphia, and Detroit indicates that, far from resisting politics, many locals were actively connected with city machines.

In the name of voluntarism, the Federation opposed not only city machines, but all forms of party loyalty.

> The American Federation of Labor has often declared and often emphasized that as our efforts are centered against all forms of industrial slavery and economic wrong, we must also direct our utmost energies to remove all forms of political servitude and party slavery. . . .

Yet, when the Socialist J. Mahlon Barnes introduced a resolution "that an organizer's commission shall not be granted to an employer of labor or to any person who occupies a public office either elective or appointive, under a political party," the AFL convention defeated it.

While the craft unions were not generally interested in national legislation they were very much involved with politics on the local level. Local unions were concerned with codes, licensing and apprenticeship laws, and other legislation; political appointments to inspectors' jobs and to other jobs less directly connected with union welfare; political pull for obtaining contracts, help in strikes, and the like; and often their share of political graft. The common theme was jobs for members; this required involvement in politics. Far from being antipolitical, many locals were intimately concerned with politics; yet they gave lip-service to the antipolitical theory of voluntarism.

These local political unionists, connected with Republican machines in Republican cities like Detroit and Philadelphia and with Democratic machines in Democratic cities like New York, supported voluntarism because it did not challenge their power. First, voluntarism required no commitment on political issues that might upset a local alliance. Of equal or greater importance, both the doctrine of voluntarism and local union officials opposed independent political action, the former because it was political, the latter because it was independent. To local unionists a national policy of nonpartisanship meant they could be Democratic in Democratic cities and Republican in Republican cities.

Consequently, a large part of the constituency of the AFL was not opposed to politics as such, but only to national politics. At the same time the local political alliances contradicted voluntarism, voluntarism protected them. Research thus far suggests that voluntarism received its prime support, not from forces that were antistate out of some pragmatic manualism, or out of antistate experience, but from forces that were very willing to use the state for their purposes, and indeed used it often.

It is arguable that a coalition of forces that were not antipolitical united behind Gompers' antipolitical philosophy because it happened to serve their interests. The use of voluntarism as an internal weapon in the fight against the Socialists also lends support to this interpretation. Voluntarism legitimized the fight for power by giving it philosophic justification. The research of Marc Karson into the role of Catholics in fighting the Socialists in the AFL is also relevant. These Catholics were not antistate at all. The more progressive, like Father John Ryan, supported social legislation, and the bulk of active Catholic trade unionists were probably involved in local politics. But the Catholics supported Gompers, and voluntarism, as alternatives to the Socialists.

CONCLUSION

Voluntarism, then, claimed to be a pragmatic philosophy which based itself on freedom and the experience of all American workers. In fact it was an abstract philosophy, which received its prime support from a constituency whose experience and interests were significantly different from that of American workers as a whole.

Internally, voluntarism meant that the leaders were free to coerce the union membership. Externally, voluntarism protected the freedom of the craft union to bargain for a seven-hour day while the unorganized workers were forced to work far longer. Externally, voluntarism also kept the leaders free from having to press for unemployment insurance while the unemployed were forced to exist—where they could—on the dole. Finally, voluntarism kept the city locals free—not free from politics, but free to form political alliances with city machines. If I have stressed the conflict of these organizational needs with broader constituency needs, this has been only to question the Perlman tradition. At times, organizational needs served constituency needs. Voluntarism, however, was above all an organizational ideology, serving organizational needs.

The Expansion of the American Labor Movement: Institutional Sources of Stimulus and Restraint

DAVID BRODY

American trade unionism experienced two growth periods: one from 1897 to 1904 when membership surged to one-tenth of the national labor force; a second from 1935 to 1945 when organization expanded to cover one-fourth of the work force, a proportion that has remained pretty much constant since then. In what ways did the structure and ideology of the labor movement account for this distinctive pattern of growth? That is the subject of the following essay. The analysis leads to two conclusions. First, a modest assessment of its role in the system gave organized labor little incentive to try to alter the larger conditions that acted on organizational growth. And, second, the setting governed union tactics, which were aggressively responsive in favorable times, rigidly restrictive in periods of adversity. Given the evident fact that the decisive factors for union expansion lay outside the labor movement, the editor should perhaps acknowledge that he wrote the essay not so much to explain *why* growth occurred as to discover *how* the labor movement shaped its organizing strategy. And this question, in turn, he hoped would throw some light on the way actions and policies arose out of basic institutional characteristics.

ON DECEMBER 29, 1932, GEORGE E. BARNETT, DEAN OF JOHNS Hopkins labor economists, delivered the presidential address before the American Economic Association. His speech had an ironic ring, for, at the close of a distinguished career, Professor Barnett was consigning the subject of his scholarship to a place of secondary interest. Trade union-

From Stephen E. Ambrose, ed., *Institutions in Modern America,* Baltimore: The Johns Hopkins University Press, 1967, pp. 11–36. Reprinted by permission of the publisher. Footnotes have been omitted except where they amplify the text.

ism, he said, was exercising "lessening importance . . . in American economic organization." Membership stood below three million, a mark passed fifteen years before. Professor Barnett traced labor's decline back beyond the great depression which was raging at the time of his address. Basic weaknesses had emerged during the previous decade, when for the first time the union movement had failed to capitalize on prosperity. Professor Barnett drew a dark conclusion: "I see no reason to believe that American trade unionism will so revolutionize itself within a short period as to become in the next decade a more potent social influence than it has been in the past decade."

Yet inside of six months organized labor was resurgent. It recovered the losses of a decade in two years, gained another three million workmen between 1935 and 1938, and reached fourteen million members in a final surge during the war years. "Measured in numbers, political influence, economic weight, or by any other yardstick," the president of the United States Chamber of Commerce acknowledged in 1944, "labor is a power in our land." It was a far cry from the future predicted by Professor Barnett in 1932.

His miscalculation suggests a way of looking at the growth of the modern labor movement. American trade unionism housed contradictory tendencies toward the unorganized—a propensity toward rigid restriction and an opposing responsive capacity for growth. The expansive tendency, rarely very marked since the early years, had fallen entirely from sight during the twenties and early thirties. Nor would a close study of trade unions have predicted the resurgence of the expansive phase. For the trigger was not in the labor movement, but in the larger environment. Professor Barnett's pessimism in 1932 was well founded (and almost uniformly shared): he could not foresee the impending turn of national events, nor, even had he done so, would the recent past have suggested the trade unions' capacity to respond to the opportunity granted by the great depression and the New Deal.

This dualism had its roots in the formative period of American unionism in the late nineteenth century. The movement shaped itself on a modest appraisal of its situation in American society. Nineteenth-century reformers had envisaged all "producers"—that is, nearly everyone—marching toward a co-operative commonwealth. Only saloonkeepers, lawyers, and stockbrokers had been excluded from the Knights of Labor. The optimism of labor reformers rested on their denial of class conflict. Trade unionists saw a harsher reality—a nation permanently divided into contending classes by the Industrial Revolution. They claimed only one group for the union movement, the wage workers, and rigidly excluded everyone else. But, if American labor was class-conscious, it was so in a peculiarly American way. In this pluralistic society, men thought of themselves not only as workers, but as Catholics, Republicans, Odd Fellows, and much else besides. Trade unionism could not contradict those other loyalties. Nor could it pursue goals other than those of concern to its members. And American workingmen were, in Selig Perlman's phrase, "job-conscious." They confined their interests, as workers, to the terms of their employment. Voluntary associations that they were, trade unions could lead only where the rank and file would follow—a narrow channel indeed.

No one saw more steadily nor better articulated the consequences of these modest circumstances than did Samuel Gompers. Not that he repudiated his youthful dreams ("I believe with the most advanced thinkers as to ultimate ends including the abolition of the wage-system," he was still saying in 1887), but he set them aside and, eventually, left them behind. They were beyond the means and will of American labor. Gompers turned to the immediate and the possible. The labor movement, he explained, attempted "to work along the lines of least resistance; to accomplish the best results in improving the condition of the working people . . . each day making it a better day than the one that had gone before. . . . And wherever that may lead . . . so far in my time and my age I decline . . . to be labelled by any particular ism." The trade unionist concerned himself only with the pursuit of "more, more, more, now."

The movement likewise tailored its methods to its limitations. Economic action, not politics, seemed labor's best hope. Given a constituency limited in numbers and in commitment, the union movement could not be very strong in the political arena. Moreover, the state—the one coercive agency in American society—posed the greatest potential danger to labor. As voluntary associations, finally, trade unions found little organizational benefit in legislative gains. Compulsory unemployment insurance, William Green once warned, would "pull at our vitals and destroy our trade union structure." Collective bargaining, on the other hand, gave unions a continuing function and a claim on the members. Nineteenth-century conditions encouraged the economic bias; industrial expansion and labor shortages had consistently favored the bargaining position of American working men. Gompers elevated these considerations into ruling principles. His doctrine of "voluntarism" located the labor movement firmly in the private sector of American life. Unions should never seek "at the hands of the government what they could accomplish by their own initiative and activities." A companion doctrine, drawn from early Marxist lessons, sustained the basic tactical position of American labor: "Economic need and economic betterment could best be served by mobilizing and controlling economic power."

"Pure and simple" unionism, as Gompers' formulation came to be known, really described a tendency rooted in American labor organization. The earliest local unions, Philip Taft has shown, devoted themselves to economic action, and quickly learned to resist the temptations of politics and reform. Starting with the International Typographical Union in 1852, local bodies of the same craft began to form national unions. It was further proof of the commitment to economic unionism. The transportation revolution was nationalizing American markets. To function effectively in the economic sphere, labor organization had to parallel that change. Thus initiated, the national unions gradually evolved the essential controls over membership standards, over strikes, and over collective bargaining. The prime institutions for economic action, the national unions became the dominant units of American trade unionism. When it was formed in 1886, the American Federation of Labor recognized their supremacy in its basic laws.

The next two decades permanently validated the trade union approach. The stubborn strain of politics and reform in American labor finally withered away with the collapse of the Knights of Labor and a series of political fiascoes. The trade unions, meanwhile, were attaining institutional stability. In the eighteen nineties they survived intact a major depression for the first time. When prosperity returned, the movement burst forward. From a base of half a million in 1897, membership more than quadrupled in five years, and collective bargaining made notable headway. An expanding future seemed to lie before a movement (as Gompers had said) "founded on eminently practical questions."

But at that point American trade unionism became the victim of a historical irony. Just as the movement crystallized on the basis of nineteenth-century conditions, its environment changed drastically. The mass production revolution occurred, sharpening management opposition to collective bargaining, increasing the means for fighting unions, and undermining the union strategy of control of the labor market. Trade unionism discovered itself barred from the heart of the American economy—the great industries characterized by mass production technology and large-scale business organization. Employer opposition quickly spread beyond these confines. In 1903 the movement came under the fire of open-shop organizations headed by the National Association of Manufacturers. Public authorities joined the attack. The courts turned their injunction powers and the Sherman Anti-Trust Act against the trade unions, blunting the force of the strike and the boycott. Gompers' fear of the state now found ample justification.

These reversals exposed an unforeseen limitation of a movement shaped by pure and simple doctrine: an incapacity to respond to adverse change.

Its modest self-assessment rendered American trade unionism essentially a passive agent in relation to its surrounding environment. Labor unions operated *in,* not *against,* the economic setting. They lacked the capacity, or even the intention, of influencing the technological change that was undermining craft union strength. The vast resources of the giant corporations posed an equal obstacle to the growth of organized labor. Yet the A.F. of L. did not lead in the antitrust movement. (Indeed, Gompers accepted business concentration as an aspect of economic evolution.) Only special circumstances and an existing bargaining relationship, such as existed in the demoralized coal and clothing industries of the nineteen twenties, spurred trade unions to a direct concern with their industrial environment.

Nor could organized labor take the more obvious path of politics to alter its environment. Legislation that might redress in a direct way the balance between labor and management—a Wagner act—was ruled out. "In the demand for collective bargaining labor has never asked that it be gained by law" was the A.F. of L. response in 1919 to a bill providing for collective bargaining in industries engaged in interstate commerce. Some issues did, of course, demand political answers. When opponents employed public weapons, labor had to defend itself by political means. Likewise, trade unionists saw the benefits of public controls over the labor supply, for example, in the restriction of immigration and the regulation of child and female labor. But even on this limited scale, the union movement scored only modest success. Trade unionism was not primarily designed for political action. Authority and money accumulated in the national unions rather than in labor's political arms—the city centrals, the state federations, the A.F. of L. itself. Organized labor lacked political means, even after its aggressive shift in 1906 from lobbying tactics to electioneering for its friends and against its enemies. The trade union environment had to be taken as it was in the early twentieth century.

That left the alternative of accommodation. A conciliatory line offered one possibility. The A.F. of L. assiduously wooed big business, first in the National Civic Federation, and then, in the nineteen twenties, in a campaign (using the model of the Baltimore and Ohio plan) for greater industrial efficiency. Neither effort had much success, as Gompers' faith in economic power should have foreseen. Not conciliation but a more intelligent response to economic reality was what offered hope for the expansion of American trade unionism. That, too, proved beyond the capacity of the labor movement in a hostile environment.

The failing was not accidental; it was firmly rooted in the foundations of American organized labor. To begin with, there was the rule of trade autonomy—that is, the sovereignty of the national unions. Beyond being a safeguard for the organizations forming the A.F. of L., trade autonomy reflected the importance of the national unions as the agencies carrying on the primary functions of the movement. They had the right, Gompers had said from the beginning, "to do as they think is just and proper in matters of their own trades, without the let or hindrance of any other body of men. . . ." The Federation, Gompers reminded the delegates in his last speech to an A.F. of L. convention, was "an organization that had no power and no authority except of a voluntary character." No one outside the power structure of the national unions—and that category included some of the men best able to do the job—had the means to organize the unorganized. Unionization depended ultimately on the national unions. And they, for reasons entirely sound from their standpoint, held back on the task.

The national unions had taken shape—the transformation of the Cigarmakers' Union in the late eighteen seventies was the model instance—as vehicles for collective bargaining and the exertion of economic force. That institutional development placed restraints on the organizing function, once a stable membership was built up, internal order created, and vested interests formed. Thereafter, unionizing activities were considered essential under only one condition—when the lack of organization threatened the status quo. But such pressure did not touch some of the strongest of trade unions. The Teamsters, the construction trades, and certain other craft unions operated in local product markets. The local unions moved heaven and earth to organize their own areas, but they did not consider it vital for local markets elsewhere to be organized nor, in their own territories, workmen of their trades whose employers did not compete with the union enterprises. The primary unions in the basic industries found sheltered spots, even if these were pitifully small, in which they could survive. Except for such fields as coal and clothing, no economic imperatives drove the national unions into unorganized areas.

Then why hold so stubbornly to jurisdictions there? In part, the national unions were merely exploiting their prerogative as autonomous organizations: no authority could force them to relinquish an established claim, nor make them answerable for how they exercised their territorial rights. The national unions were also motivated by more positive considerations. The unorganized jurisdictions were filled with potential dues-paying members (which hence had a property value akin to a natural resource) and in some instances had strategic importance. The United Brotherhood of Carpenters fought relentlessly to secure jurisdiction over the entire wood industry, destroying the vigorous Amalgamated Wood Workers in the process. The objective was not so much to bring in the woodworkers as to "police" the industry. The Carpenters wanted, first, to protect their jobs should technological change shift work into the mills, and, second, to control the suppliers of unionized construction markets. So the national unions blocked any transfer of jurisdiction over workmen whom they lacked compelling reasons to organize.

Further calculations tipped the scales of tough-minded trade unionists against acting without an imperative reason. Finances had become of first importance to the functioning of labor unions. Defense funds, intricate revenue systems, and an accounting mentality had developed. Should money be diverted from regular purposes to new areas? Would the probable advantages to the existing membership justify the expenditure? The internal structure, reflecting the local market fields in which many A.F. of L. unions operated, often left much authority and income in the hands of the local unions and district bodies. Would they support organizing activities of little direct concern to them? The unions had evolved a career leadership and a one-party political system. Might not an influx of new members, especially those not drawn from a union's normal area of operation, endanger internal stability?

The list of questions lengthened. The organizing drives in mass production industries demanded a joint effort. Would other national unions co-operate and carry a fair share of the work? (The disastrous steel drive of 1919 suggested the problems in this area.) Trade unions, as voluntary associations, depended on rank and file loyalty. The unorganized were largely recent immigrants and Negroes. Might they not alienate the native-born unionists? Could mass production workers show the discipline and order essential for rational strike action and collective bargaining? (A long train of union defeats indicated how difficult it was to control freshly organized industrial workers.)

These hard questions did not all bear or bear with equal weight on every decision involving non-union ground. But responsible leaders had always to strike a balance between the narrow interests of their existing organizations and the claims of the unorganized. In an era when, in any case, the odds were weighted heavily against success, that calculation restrained the national unions as organizing agencies.

So Professor Barnett rightly despaired of American trade unionism in 1932. The movement seemed locked to the skilled occupations, and exerted power in but a handful of industries. During the twenties only the building trades flourished. Between 1920 and 1926, thirty-three unions, primarily in manufacturing, shrank in membership by nearly 60 per cent. Nor was there any sign of an inner revolution. One observer in 1926 found most labor leaders "a curious blending of defeatism with complacency." A harsher critic in 1929 dismissed the A.F. of L. as "a life raft—though now beginning to get waterlogged—for skilled labor." Three years of depression reduced the movement by another half-million members and rendered even the strongest unions ineffective in collective bargaining. At the end of 1932, as Professor Barnett observed, the labor movement, seemingly, faced a dark future.

The next months abruptly transformed the trade union environment. The depression finally broke down the acquiescent relationship fostered by welfare capitalism and aroused industrial workers to action. During the early period of the N.R.A., a spontaneous push for organization developed. It was a sight, said William Green, "that even the old, tried veterans of our movement never saw before." The depression also created a new political situation. Administrations came to power in Washington and in key states which, both from conviction and expediency, championed the cause of labor. Among the benefits to the unions, none held greater importance than the legislation that granted new rights and privileges to labor. The rank and file upheaval and political changes, together with the economic impact of the depression, cut down the defenses of capital. Even the mightiest of corporations became vulnerable to unionization during the thirties.

The labor movement was the beneficiary, not the agent, of the sudden turn in its fortunes. Only in politics did trade unions contribute—and even there but modestly—to the alteration of the environment. But this activated within the movement powerful pressures for expansion. To have attempted to unionize the basic industries earlier, John L. Lewis admitted in 1935, "would have been suicide for organized labor and would have resulted in complete failure. But now, the time is ripe; and now the time to do these things is here. Let us do them."

That decision, it is essential to see, sprang from the logic of trade unionism no less than had the opposite conclusion of earlier years. John L. Lewis was drawn directly from the pure and simple tradition of the American labor movement. He represented, one writer noted in 1925, "the older type of labor executive, autocratic, more aggressive than penetrating, unreceptive to the new principle[s], a protagonist of simple unionism." Conservative in politics, dictatorial as president of the United Mine Workers, conventional in collective bargaining despite the collapse of the coal trade, Lewis seemed in the twenties, as one observer wrote, "the grand walking delegate, the glorified organizer, the perfect boss in American labor." Yet John L. Lewis was the man who instantly sprang to the head of the group pressing for action after the start of the New Deal. "It's middling tough for one who fought John L. so long and bitterly to pay this tribute," confessed a labor journalist in 1933, "but give the devil his dues. John turned out to be the only archangel among the angels with fallen arches of the A.F. of L. crowd." Ambition and personal drive assuredly contributed to Lewis' apparent transformation—he was, as Francis Biddle later said, very nearly a great man—but his efforts were wholly explicable in trade union terms. That statement holds also for Sidney Hillman, David Dubinsky, Charles Howard, and the lesser men who gathered around Lewis. Observing them at the end of 1933, David Saposs found "no ideological difference distinguishing them from the old guard. . . . They differ from the old guard on the best way to take advantage of the opportunity presented by government intervention. . . ."

The industrial union group was responding, first of all, to the historical sense of obligation to the unorganized. Gompers had always insisted that the A.F. of L. spoke for all wage earners, not just union men, and he had never ceased working for the spread of labor organization. Even when it grew remote from the concerns of many craft union leaders, they never could deny the goal of organizing the unorganized. The low point came in the twenties, when prosperity and welfare capitalism began to undermine confidence in the social value of labor organization. The depression revived labor's sense of indignation. In 1932, the A.F. of L. came out for public unemployment insurance, a startling departure from the rule of voluntarism. The mild William Green astonished the entire country when he threatened "forceful methods" to shorten hours and increase wages. "We have simply come to what we are determined shall be the end of the road of suffering." That sentiment grew especially compelling among the advocates of industrial unionism. "The labor movement is organized upon a principle that the strong shall help the weak," John L. Lewis pleaded before the A.F. of L. convention of 1935. "Isn't it right that we should contribute something of our own strength . . . toward those less fortunately situated. . . . Organize the unorganized and in so doing you make the American Federation of Labor the greatest instrumentality that has ever been forged in the history of modern civilization to befriend the cause of humanity and champion human rights."

But trade unionists had always held realism in higher regard than compassion. The American setting denied them the luxury of sacrificing power for ideals. The industrial unionists shared that tough-minded assumption. "A union should be regarded as . . . progressive when it brings about a new condition in industry through the exercise of its power," Sidney Hillman had argued in 1928. "Policy and strategy are only the means to the end, and the end is the realization of power for the movement." Union men of vision had always insisted that greater organization would strengthen all the unions in the movement, and now so did the industrial unionists. But equally important was the narrower calculation habitual to the national unions. The United Mine Workers had just survived a harrowing decade, in which its troubles had derived largely from the competition of non-union coal fields. Now, rescued by the National Industrial Recovery Act, Lewis was determined to secure his union from that threat, and his objective required the unionization of the steel industry. John Brophy, Lewis' lieutenant, emphasized the connection in his memoirs: "Steel was the key to understanding Lewis' policy; the mine workers would never be safe until steel was unionized. . . . Lewis and the UMW, intent on steel, were driven to create the CIO, because there was no other way to get the job in steel done." The Clothing Workers and the Ladies' Garment Workers were similarly situated. Both waged a constant battle against non-union competition, and hence saw specific benefits in the organization of related industries. So the narrow considerations of pure and simple unionism weighed heavily in the thinking of the industrial unionists.

Political change added another element to their calculations. Trade unionists had always concentrated on economic power, and, whether A.F. of L. or C.I.O., they continued to do so in the thirties. But politics was now looming larger. For one thing, much was at stake. The depression had drawn the government decisively into labor's sphere. On the other hand, political patterns had altered. The New Deal was responsive to organized labor, provided only that its voice was strong. The automobile code had worked out badly, Lewis observed, because labor weakness (in this case, the lack of a national union) permitted "the Recovery Administration and the White House to make decisions without fear of any successful challenge from the American Federation of Labor." The industrial unionists were particularly sensitive to political factors partly because of their experience in Washington during the N.R.A. period, partly from the special need for government regulation in their industries, and in some cases from past conviction. A large-scale labor movement seemed to them essential to meet the political demands of the Roosevelt era.

Not all trade unionists responded to these calculations. Older restraints operated in key craft organizations and, indeed, grew more deeply entrenched in the face of challenge. Between 1933 and 1935 their contribution, either in the way of money or co-operation, fell short of past attempts to organize the basic industries, and they embraced more stubbornly the principles of trade autonomy and exclusive jurisdiction. The craft unions would not countenance the bypassing of ineffective unions with major jurisdictions, nor would they themselves forego their claims to men in the mass production fields. "We are not going to desert the fundamental principles on which [the craft unions] have lived and are living to help you organize men who have never been organized," Daniel Tobin of the Teamsters bluntly told John L. Lewis at a climactic meeting in May, 1935.

That obstinacy only revealed the intensity of the expansionist impulse activated by the changed environment. "We were all convinced," John Brophy recalled of a strategy meeting held soon after, "that in the temper of the times, there was a great opportunity to push forward . . . that if the delay was continued too long, it would mean the opportunity would run out on us, and we would lose a chance that only comes once in a long while." To exploit it, the industrial unionists finally resorted to independent action.

Violating though it did labor's cardinal rule against dual unionism, that undertaking was entirely logical from a trade union standpoint. Lewis insisted that his were "not the objectives of someone else, but the declared objectives of the American Federation of Labor. . . ." Only one question concerned him: what would work? For mass production workers, Lewis answered, only industrial unions. The issue of structure no longer held ideological significance, as it earlier had among radicals bent on transforming the labor movement. In the thirties the matter became a practical one. Industrial workers—"mass-minded," as William Green described them—resisted division into separate unions. Nor had this arrangement in the past provided the degree of unity that seemed essential in confronting the giant corporations. So rubber, steel, and auto unions had to be formed on an industrial basis. Entirely pragmatic in his view of the structural issue, Lewis in late 1934 tried to make a bargain that would preserve the essentials: let industrial jurisdictions be granted on a temporary basis; the craft unions that so desired could exercise their claims later, when division would not endanger the mass production unions.

From that point on, considerations of power—as characteristic as Lewis' pragmatism in the labor movement—dominated and forced the dispute over structure to the point of an open split. The craft unions, after seeming to agree, quickly backed away from Lewis' proposition. Could they exercise their jurisdictions after unionization had occurred on an industrial basis? Not if the new unions were strong enough to prevent it. For all the attention to legality, in the end power counted in the labor movement. So the craft unions excluded specific groups from the jurisdictions of the Auto Workers and the Rubber Workers at meetings of the A.F. of L. Executive Council in early 1935. They had enough votes later in the year to ratify that action at the fateful A.F. of L. convention in Atlantic City. But a ballot could not settle this issue. The Lewis group had a vital interest and the means to pursue it. In the past, the labor movement had always given in to that combination—hence, among other things, the granting of industrial jurisdiction to the Mine Workers in 1901. Now in the thirties a unique situation faced the A.F. of L.: a confrontation of two power blocs with vital interests. Given the fact that Lewis considered it essential to organize mass production workers, his decision to ignore the A.F. of L. resolution against industrial unionism was sound from a trade union standpoint. Nor, curiously, was it out of character for craft chieftains such as William Hutcheson—himself a master of *machtpolitik*—to raise their hands in horror over Lewis' violation of majority rule and exclusive jurisdiction. In a labor movement lacking a strong central authority, legality and power politics existed side by side. The only surprising feature was that, without much regard for the constitutional niceties, the craft unions should have carried their disapproval to the extreme of reading the industrial union group out of the American Federation of Labor and so transformed the Committee for Industrial Organization into a rival federation.

Free as it was to experiment, the C.I.O. actually drew heavily on the strengths and practices of American trade unionism. The organizing drives, of course, posed special, and to some degree new, problems. The mass production workers were aroused; their Negro and immigrant elements injected further resentments and sensitivities; and the Wagner act gave them a free choice of union representation. In this situation, fresh tactics necessarily emerged, and the C.I.O. had special advantages in the struggle to win rank and file support. Yet the C.I.O. was not departing from basic trade union patterns. With the exception of the major innovation of the "organizing committee" (such as the Steel Workers Organizing Committee), the structural arrangements followed those already in existence, and much of the C.I.O. effectiveness depended on traditional characteristics. American labor unions emphasized financial strength, so the C.I.O. could throw funds into organizing work on a massive scale; they employed a staff of professionals, so a cadre of organizers was immediately available; they had autocratic leadership, so the allocation of their resources raised no effective opposition. "We're in a position to throw our weight about," John L. Lewis told his subordinates after the United Mine Workers had re-established itself in the coal industry. "We have some resources. We have some money and some manpower to put into a struggle of this kind."

A final ingredient of C.I.O. success derived from the established movement—namely, an ability to exploit the American left wing. The C.I.O. attracted able leaders who, from a variety of standpoints, rejected the standing order. Some of Lewis' former enemies, such as John Brophy, Adolph Germer, and Powers Hapgood, swallowed their bitterness and followed Lewis now because he seemed the key to social change. Germer, who had been secretary of the Socialist Party, quit because, as he explained, it was a time for action, not talk. Another socialist, who also had begun to concentrate on union affairs, agreed "that working in an economic organization we are likely to accomplish more now than working in the party, as it is now constituted."[1] The moderate American left had always been drawn to the trade union movement when it gave promise of effectiveness—as it did in the thirties. The other side of the coin was that left-wingers were welcomed into the C.I.O. That, too, was in keeping with the trade union past. As a voluntary association in a pluralistic society, the labor movement necessarily judged men by performance, not by belief or by other affiliations. Participants had only to adhere to the code of priorities: while in the role of trade unionists, they had to place union objectives first. Socialists had functioned in the labor movement on this basis for many years. John L. Lewis was willing to accept even Communists, not only because (as he said) he felt confident that he could control them, but because the labor movement could control them: their participation depended on devotion to trade union, that is, collective bargaining, objectives. The Cold War subsequently created international issues of greater moment to labor, and resulted in the expulsion of Communist-dominated unions from the C.I.O. in 1949.[2] But during the organizing period, for reasons fixed in the trade union past, the C.I.O. received a mighty contribution from left-wingers for its non-radical purposes.

After the great victories against General Motors and United States Steel in early 1937, quick progress to complete unionization was anticipated. The road, however, proved unexpectedly difficult. New Deal legislation and depression conditions permitted organizations to gain a foothold, but not to secure themselves, in the basic industries. Only further environmental changes—the return of prosperity after 1939 and then the emergency conditions of World War II—made collective bargaining effective

[1] There had also been a radical left wing which had always insisted on dual unionism, i.e., no participation in the conservative movement. By the thirties, the radical left had been supplanted, except for fragments, by the Communist Party; and its relations with organized labor were determined, not by the historical positions of the American left, but by instructions from Moscow. As it happened, the Party reverted to a policy of boring from within in 1935, and its members became available to the C.I.O.

[2] An essential distinction must be drawn here between attitudes toward Communists based on internal politics and on fundamental ideological differences. The Communists were fought within C.I.O. unions on the former grounds (in fact, Lewis had long since barred them from the United Mine Workers) because the Communists operated as disciplined factions in the struggle for internal control. The issue was over power, not over basic policies. When the Communists won out, they did not reorient their organizations away from trade union objectives—hence the successful union careers of men like Harry Bridges, Julius Emspak, and Ben Gold. And where they did, as in the United Automobile Workers and the National Maritime Union in the mid-forties, the Communists quickly lost their hold.

and completed the unionizing process. By 1946, the C.I.O. had come close to its goal in the mass production sector of the economy.

That achievement, fundamental as it was, did not exhaust labor's capacity to expand in a favorable environment. Another pattern of growth, more conventional initially but perhaps of larger significance in the long run, accompanied the triumph of industrial organization. The A.F. of L. was itself expanding. It increased just as rapidly as did the C.I.O. for the first decade after the split, and then in the later forties began to outdistance its smaller rival. By the time of the merger in 1955, the A.F. of L. represented over ten million men, the C.I.O. five million.

Mass production industry had made a peculiarly difficult demand on the labor movement—namely, that established national unions subordinate their own institutional interests and encourage an organizational growth that would not accrue to them. Only the men initiating the C.I.O. had been able to jump that gap—to think, as Sidney Hillman said, "in terms of the whole labor movement." The others continued to concentrate first of all on their own national unions, as the structure and logic of American trade unionism had always dictated. But that narrower focus did not render the A.F. of L. unions ineffectual; on the contrary, after 1935 it stimulated expansion on a vast scale within the existing framework of the national unions. Between 1936 and 1941, the Machinists grew from 105,000 to 284,000, the building trades unions from 650,000 to 893,000. The Teamsters, never larger than 100,000 before 1933, reached 170,000 in 1936, 530,000 in 1941 and 1,300,000 in 1955. Of the six biggest national unions in the early sixties, four had been old-line A.F. of L. unions —Teamsters, Machinists, Electrical Workers, Carpenters.

Initially, these craft unions had seen no more than an opportunity to fill in their basic occupational jurisdictions. They had opposed the industrial union group so stubbornly because at last the craft workers in mass production industries had seemed accessible to them. But then a quiet revolution occurred: A.F. of L. unions began to expand beyond their favored job groups. The exclusive view continued to prevail in some quarters. "No organizing campaign was put into effect by our International office to recruit membership in wholesale lots," the Bricklayers' officers assured the membership in 1938. "We insisted that our unions function for the benefit of those who had remained loyal to the organization through times of stress. . . ." But new conditions increasingly overwhelmed that old-line viewpoint. The calculations remained characteristically trade union, but the conclusion now pointed in the direction of expansion—toward bringing in lower paid men working by the side of skilled men, toward moving into related areas hitherto neglected, and, finally, even toward including accessible workers wholly unconnected with the main jurisdictions.

Part of the expansionist logic was simply opportunistic. Men who would pay dues could be had for the taking. Thus the explanation of a vice president of the butchers' union: "I couldn't see much future in just working on Meat Cutters and Packing House Workers, so I started on a campaign on the Creamery, Poultry, and Egg Houses." For some union leaders, especially of the younger generation, more membership provided its own justification. Economic change, as always, played a part in reshaping jurisdictional interests. The Teamsters, for example, covered only local delivery drivers at the start of the thirties. During that decade, intercity trucking became a major industry: ton-mile traffic tripled between 1935 and 1941. Although President Dan Tobin preferred to hold to the specialized local drivers—the so-called crafts—younger leaders pushed the union into this immense field, which employed more than a million men in 1941. In this instance, expansion promised added strategic advantages for the existing membership. In other cases, industrial change made growth necessary for defensive reasons. The butchers' union, which had limited itself in the retail field to meat cutters, began to organize food clerks, partly to protect the skilled men from changes growing out of the chain-store system and the self-service supermarket. The defensive reasons for expansion derived less, however, from economic developments than from the challenge of the C.I.O.

In 1934 the International Association of Machinists received jurisdiction over aircraft workers. At first the union acknowledged the rights of other organizations to men of their trades in the plants. By 1938, the I.A.M. was battling the C.I.O. for the aircraft workers and organizing "on the only basis that could be successful and that is, taking in all mechanics. . . . If this method is interfered with, the Machinists could not continue to organize in this industry." So, ironically, competition from the C.I.O. made this most stubborn opponent of industrial unionism in 1935 almost immediately an industrial union in some areas. By 1952, over a third of the Machinists' membership was classified as production workers, and the next year the union dropped entirely the distinction in membership between journeymen and others. It had cut loose entirely from its craft union origins.

To avert the C.I.O., A.F. of L. unions moved also into neglected related fields. The United Brotherhood of Carpenters, for example, had successfully laid claim to the entire wood industry before World War I, but, despite greater capacity than any other union for effective action in the pre-New Deal period, this powerful craft union had actually not bothered about the woodworkers. When organization began almost spontaneously in the northwest during the N.R.A., the Carpenters accepted the wood-workers reluctantly as second-class participants in the organization. ("B" membership, involving lower dues, fewer benefits, and restricted political rights, was a standard way of handling new groups incorporated into A.F. of L. unions.) As soon as the C.I.O. invaded the Pacific lumber industry, that indifference faded; the woodworkers could not be permitted to organize independent of the carpenters. A union fight of unparalleled violence and intensity ensued, even involving a naval battle between A.F. of L. and C.I.O. boats patrolling the waters around the sawmills. As the C.I.O. expanded beyond the original basic industries, other A.F. of L. unions were likewise prompted to enter related fields: thus, initially to forestall the C.I.O., the Teamsters began to take in warehousemen; the Electricians, utility workers; the construction trades, residential building workers.

The expansion of A.F. of L. unions grew, finally, from the discovery of special organizing advantages. Success was rarely forthcoming at the core of mass production industry. The C.I.O. excelled at organizing the great plants, the large industrial centers, the major firms, the points where the task was to win rank and file support and then utilize the democratic procedures of the Wagner act to acquire representational rights. But there remained a vast field outside or peripheral to the mass production sector that was susceptible to—indeed, better suited to—the tactics of the A.F. of L. unions. For one thing, they tended to have a decentralized structure. The local unions, established everywhere, gave access to the dispersed parts of the economy. And, with a large degree of autonomy, the locals had both the means and desire to carry on organizing work. A further superiority became apparent after the great surge of organization. The decentralized A.F. of L. nationals did not have to service their locals intensively, as did C.I.O. industrial unions, and so had a greater part of their income free for organizing work. Local vitality, although rarely noticed, made a steady contribution of immense importance to the growth of the A.F. of L.

As important as decentralization was the strategic power available to some organizations. Once the Teamsters began to incorporate highway drivers, the union held a powerful weapon for coercive organizing. By compelling union trucking firms not to transfer freight to non-union lines, the Teamsters could force the latter to recognize them and so extend their organization with vast efficiency. Using "leap-frog organizing" (as they called it), the Teamsters in the late thirties jumped from Chicago to St. Louis and Joplin, Missouri, from Minneapolis to Kansas City and Omaha. The intercity trucking industry was thus swiftly organized. The same leverage was then applied to local truckers, and finally to a wide range of businesses dependent on truck deliveries. The Teamsters rendered vital help to unions organizing retail stores, bakeries, laundries, and a host of small manufacturing plants, and then gradually began to retain these diversified groups within the organization. "Once you have the road men," Jimmy Hoffa boasted, "you can have the local cartage, and once you have the local cartage, you can get anyone you want."

While not so strategically located as the Teamsters, other A.F. of L. unions made good use of pressure tactics. In the fierce fight for the northwest lumber industry, the Carpenters refused to handle wood produced in C.I.O. plants. "Why don't [the C.I.O. leaders] admit that a union is strong or weak depending on its power to boycott efficiently?" crowed the United Brotherhood. The boycott enabled the Carpenters to recapture a substantial part of the Pacific industry, despite lack of popularity and resourceful opposition from the C.I.O. union. The retail branch of the A.F. of L. butchers' union exerted the same kind of pressure on meat processing plants, and to some extent so did other craft unions moving into manufacturing fields. Although the techniques varied immensely, and included collusion as well as force, strategic A.F. of L. unions followed the essential approach of concentrating their organizing efforts on employers no less than on workers. Notwithstanding the fact that it conflicted with the democratic policy of the Wagner act to give workers a free choice on union representation, this tactic was fostered by many developments in the thirties, above all by legal sanctions permitting organizational picketing and the secondary boycott.

So the favorable environment evoked from the labor movement two patterns of growth. The dramatic response involved the creation of industrial unions for the basic industries. Some old-line unions meanwhile evolved into diversified organizations especially effective at reaching the less accessible workmen outside the mass production sector of the economy. These two approaches had never been entirely distinct, and they overlapped even more as the industrial unions exhausted their main fields. Together, they lifted the labor movement to the level of eighteen million members by 1955 (three million outside the A.F. of L. and C.I.O.). American trade unionism had found within itself capacities for expansion unanticipated in the trying years prior to the great depression and the New Deal.

In the end, this analysis returns to its starting point. Professor Barnett had foreseen a diminishing future for the labor movement in 1932. During recent years, his gloomy words have found an echo among union experts. In 1953 the labor editor of *Fortune,* Daniel Bell, announced that "U.S. labor has lost the greatest single dynamic any movement can have —a confidence that it is going to get bigger. Organized labor has probably passed its peak strength." Although his argument was disputed at the time, Bell's prediction proved to be shrewd and accurate. During the rest of the fifties the increase of union membership—at an average rate of roughly one hundred thousand per year—was not great enough even to maintain the unions' share of the total labor force.[3] Trade unionism seemed to be hardening. Its ideas lacked freshness, its policies popular appeal. Age crept up even on those new-style leaders like Walter Reuther, who were raised in the great upheaval of the thirties. When Congressional investigation revealed undemocratic internal politics and widespread corrupt practices, the final signs of labor's declining vitality seemed clear. Recent criticisms recall the harshness of pre-New Deal observers of trade unionism.

[3] Irving Bernstein took issue with Bell in a fine article which, while it could not negate the accuracy of Bell's prediction, did demonstrate conclusively the lack of correlation between union growth and the major indices of economic activity ("The Growth of American Unions," *American Economic Review*, XLIV [June, 1954], 301–318). In a subsequent article in 1961, Bernstein argued that the labor movement had actually turned in a creditable growth performance since the end of World War II. He attempted to answer the "saturationist" position that labor had reached the limit of the organizable part of the economy by pointing to the growth of unions in the non-manufacturing sector and by arguing that women, the South, agriculture, and white-collar work should not be written off as impervious to trade unionism. And he presented a new series that showed greater growth since 1945 than had appeared in earlier statistics:

Year	Membership	% of Civilian Labor Force
1945	13,379,000	24.8
1946	13,648,000	23.7
1947	14,845,000	24.7
1949	14,960,000	24.1
1950	14,751,000	23.4
1951	16,211,000	25.8
1952	16,730,000	26.6
1953	17,884,000	28.0
1954	17,757,000	27.5
1955	17,749,000	27.0
1956	18,477,000	27.4
1957	18,430,000	27.1
1958	18,081,000	26.3
1959	18,452,000	26.6
1960	18,607,000	26.2

Although these statistics do show an impressive increase of 4.5 million members between 1945 and 1953, primarily during the Korean War, since then Bernstein's figures show an average increase of only one hundred thousand a year, and the percentage of union members in the labor force slipped by almost two points ("The Growth of American Unions, 1945–1960," *Labor History*, II [Spring, 1961], 131–157).

Obviously, the movement has not come full circle. Organized labor is incomparably stronger today than it was thirty-five years ago. Powerful labor unions now share in the basic decisions that govern the economy. The A.F. of L.-C.I.O. exerts an influence in politics beyond anything envisaged by Samuel Gompers. In its internal affairs, organized labor has become more flexible and realistic. It would be hard to imagine the A.F. of L.-C.I.O. being held back, as was the A.F. of L. before 1935, by rigid notions of jurisdictional rights and trade autonomy. And the organizing techniques devised by A.F. of L. unions continue to have a significant measure of success in non-manufacturing areas.

Yet as a whole, the labor movement finds itself at a standstill. Despite the important differences, the situation today has an underlying similarity with that before the depression. Growth has stopped because organized labor has again run into an unfavorable environment. And, as earlier, the movement is stymied. Its greater strength notwithstanding, it still lacks the capacity to change the adverse environment. It cannot forestall the new technology that is cutting into its base in many fields; at best, it hopes to protect those of its members caught by change. It cannot reverse legislative and court decisions, beginning with the Taft-Hartley act, that have taken away some key advantages. It can do little to change the circumstances that make the major unorganized areas—the South, agriculture, white-collar work—unresponsive to trade unionism. Nor, on the other hand, has the labor movement shown much greater ability to alter itself in ways that would permit it to grow *within* the contemporary environment than it had before the depression. As earlier, organized labor has found no answer to adversity.

The foregoing line of analysis does suggest two predictions beyond what Professor Barnett saw in 1932. Should the environment become more favorable—possibly as a result of racial progress in the South, new labor patterns in agriculture, automation in white-collar fields, or, more dramatically, from political or economic upheaval—the labor movement would show itself able to seize the opportunity. It is equally probable that, should another breakthrough occur, trade unionism would not depart from the basic direction charted by Samuel Gompers any more than the movement did in the thirties. By drawing these two lessons from recent labor history, of course, a third is ignored: namely, not to make predictions and so to avoid being found in error, as is the case with Professor Barnett here, by future historians.

Unions and the Black Community

RAY MARSHALL

In the recent history of the American labor movement, no issue has attracted greater attention than the problem of racial discrimination. It is a subject (like that of the tactics of unionization) properly studied in light of the basic characteristics of the movement. From the outset, the American Federation of Labor enunciated the principle of complete equalitarianism (just as it asserted the goal of organizing all workers). But, given its voluntaristic rules and its respect for the power realities, the federation accommodated itself to the actuality of American racism: it countenanced discriminatory practices by the affiliated national unions and organized workers on a segregated basis. On the other hand, when more was to be gained from following an equalitarian line, segments of the labor movement—the United Mine Workers, for instance—always did so. This was preeminently the case when the task was undertaken to organize the mass-production workers during the New Deal. Not surprisingly, the Congress of Industrial Organizations committed itself wholeheartedly to racial equality. But, holding as it did the same basic trade-union outlook as the AFL, the CIO began to trim its sails in the face of changing organizational needs. In the past decade, different winds have sprung up—rising black militancy, governmental pressures, aroused public sentiment—and we are seeing the labor movement moving predictably, if painfully, to accommodate itself to the new situation, ultimately, one hopes, to match in practice the principles it has always held in the abstract. This is what Ray Marshall, a leading student of the subject, relates in this summary essay, without, however, quite making explicit the connection between labor practices and the underlying characteristics of business unions.

From Ray Marshall, "Unions and Negro Community," *The Industrial and Labor Relations Review*, XVII (January, 1964), pp. 179–191, 193, 199–202. Reprinted by permission of the publisher. Footnotes have been omitted except where they amplify the text.

THE RECENT ATTACKS ON UNIONS BY VARIOUS NEGRO AND CIVIL rights organizations raise the question of the future of Negro-labor relations and of the consequences of these developments for industrial relations. Indeed, it seems generally conceded that the "civil rights" question is one of the main unsolved problems facing American unions. Its solution is believed to have important applications for the survival and growth of unions, not only because of the importance for the labor movement of gaining the political and economic support of minority groups, but also because this is an important moral question which influences public opinion of unions at a time when they are losing prestige and strength. The basic purpose of this article is to analyze the current schism between unions and the Negro community against the background of historical Negro-labor relations.

EARLY BEGINNINGS

Like most other racial problems, the union-Negro conflict had its roots in slavery and Reconstruction, though this was considered to be mainly a southern problem until Negroes started migrating out of the South in large numbers. This migration was accelerated by World War I, and has continued since. Indeed, in 1963 a majority of Negroes probably live outside the states which made up the Confederacy.[1]

Following the Civil War, unions adopted a variety of practices with respect to Negroes. Apparently almost every southern union having the power to do so excluded Negroes from membership. But in some cases Negro workers were too numerous to be excluded entirely, because the white locals found their strikes broken by them or discovered that Negro competition would jeopardize union conditions. Consequently, central labor unions and organizations of longshoremen, musicians, carpenters, and bricklayers took Negroes into segregated locals. The American Federation of Labor adopted a policy of organizing Negro workers into federal locals attached directly to the federation, a technique which proved unsatisfactory to the national unions, which lost dues, and the Negroes, who were inadequately represented. Several AFL organizations had constitu-

---

[1] The South's proportion of the nation's nonwhites declined from 88% in 1910 to 85% in 1920 and 74% in 1930; in 1940, 73% of the nation's nonwhites lived in the former Confederate states plus Kentucky and Oklahoma, as compared with only 51% in 1960. Since this trend has continued and since a large proportion of nonwhites in the South are Negroes, it seems safe to conclude that today less than half of the Negroes in the United States reside in the South.

tional race bars or were known to exclude Negroes by other means. Other unions gradually abandoned exclusion in favor of auxiliary locals, a device Negroes bitterly protested, because they paid dues but were represented (or better, misrepresented) by white officers. The auxiliary local was gradually abolished after the 1930's because various laws and court decisions held it to be incompatible with union security provisions.

Sometimes the Negro workers themselves insisted that they be placed in segregated (not auxiliary) locals because they were afraid they would be discriminated against by whites, who were usually in the majority, if the unions were integrated. There were some cases where unions started out integrated, but split for this reason. In other instances, however, Negroes would have preferred integration because they had inadequate job opportunities on a segregated basis. This was particularly true of the Carpenters, who accepted Negro members but, until 1963, had a policy of forming segregated locals in the South.

While a certain stability of union-Negro relationships was established in the South by the time the Congress of Industrial Organizations was formed in the 1930's, the migration of Negroes to the North did not take place peacefully. Indeed, Negroes were frequently barred from craft unions in the North which admitted them in the South. This was true, for instance, of bricklayers, longshoremen, cement finishers, roofers, plasterers, and carpenters. Colored workers usually took jobs in disagreeable occupations in northern automobile foundries, steel mills, packinghouses, coal mines, and railroads, and frequently engendered hostility from white workers by entering these jobs as strikebreakers. Moreover, some Negro leaders advised Negro workers to remain in the South where they would have better job opportunities, and a number of very bloody race riots in northern cities during and after World War I resulted partly from white resentment at the importation of Negro strikebreakers. The important 1919 steel strike was broken in large measure due to the almost complete lack of Negro support in many areas. Outstanding Negro leaders like Booker T. Washington adopted the position that Negroes should ally themselves with employers against unions and white workers, an attitude some AFL leaders used to justify their racial policies.

Thus, while the AFL itself adopted an equalitarian racial position from the very beginning, it either could not or would not prohibit discrimination by its affiliates, whose practices contributed to the Negro's low economic status. AFL leaders justified the federation's position on the antiunion attitudes of Negro leaders and the use of Negro strikebreakers, as well as the AFL's lack of power to deal with discriminating affiliates. By the time the CIO was formed, therefore, there was considerable hostility between unions and the Negro community.

THE CIO

Union racial practices were very important in the rivalry between the AFL and the CIO during the union upsurge of the 1930's. The CIO took full advantage of the AFL's unfavorable racial image to organize thousands of Negro workers in the coal and ore mining, steel, auto, rubber, and packinghouse industries which formed the backbone of the CIO. Indeed, it is probably true that these industries could not have been organized without Negro support, because Negroes frequently formed the balance of power between the union and nonunion whites. Moreover, CIO leaders had important political objectives, which required the support of the Negro community. It therefore became imperative for the CIO to change the traditional antiunion and Republican attitudes of Negro community leaders.

In order to accomplish its objectives, the CIO adopted many programs to gain a favorable image in Negro communities. These programs included financial contributions to organizations like the National Association for the Advancement of Colored People and Negro churches and newspapers, the adoption of equalitarian racial resolutions, the use of Negroes to organize in Negro communities, the creation of the Committee to Abolish Racial Discrimination, and interlocking officials between unions and such organizations as the NAACP and the National Urban League.

Before the CIO was formed, national NAACP leaders were very skeptical of the AFL's organizing activities because, according to Roy Wilkins, then the Association's assistant secretary, "We strongly suspect, although we cannot prove, the AF of L unions have attempted to use Section 7-A [of the National Recovery Act] to drive Negroes out of occupations. . . ." Wilkins added:

> It is not easy for an Association which knows so intimately the raw deals that have been given Negro labor by the AF of L to get out and shout from the housetops to Negro workers urging them to affiliate. At the same time we realize that affiliation would be best for all concerned provided one did not have just as great a battle after getting in the union as one had on the outside.

With the formation of the CIO, however, the NAACP realized that Negroes had an opportunity to ally themselves with a new, different, and perhaps powerful labor movement and consequently actively supported the new organization. In September 1936, for example, *Crisis*, the official organ of the NAACP, proposed that Negroes join the CIO if it followed the racial policies of the United Mine Workers. (The UMW, the main organization supporting the CIO, had long followed equalitarian policies in organizing Negroes in the North and the South.) *Crisis* also sought to overcome Negro opposition to the CIO by declaring:

> In this struggle of labor to organize and win the right of collective bargaining, it is fitting that the Negro workers be represented in the front line trenches. . . . They have everything to gain and nothing to lose by affiliation with the CIO and if they fight now, side by side with their fellow workers, when the time comes to divide up the benefits they can demand their share.

However, Negro leaders who had formed close working relations with employers like Henry Ford in Detroit did not easily surrender the advantages of these alliances for the uncertain benefits to be derived from an emerging power center. As a result, many NAACP branches at first opposed CIO as well as AFL unions; local branches in Chicago, Indianapolis, and Detroit being particularly outspoken in their opposition. At the NAACP's 1936 annual conference in Detroit, a dispute developed over whether or not to invite Homer Martin, president of the United Auto Workers, as speaker. Several Detroit Negro ministers who had received financial support from the Ford Motor Company objected to including labor representatives on the program. The conference finally adopted a resolution which suggested to

> Negro workers that they go into no labor organization blindly but that they instead appraise critically the motives and practices of all labor unions and that they bear their full share of activity and responsibility in building of a more just and more intelligent labor union.

Crisis argued concerning this conference, that "to have held a national conference and ignored discussion of the biggest labor movement in a quarter century would have been a farce deserving nationwide condemnation."

The National Urban League also established close working relations with the CIO. Indeed, the NUL had sought to form a better relationship with the AFL as early as 1919, but the AFL gave the League little active help or encouragement in these efforts. Moreover, several of the League's local affiliates had reputations as strikebreaking organizations. During the ferment of the New Deal days, the League urged Negroes, through Negro Workers' Councils, to join unions. It stated that Negroes should

> . . . seek union membership and maintain it, even when their presence was undesired by White officers or members of a local union. The Urban League meantime hammered at the attention of labor leadership, warn-

ing them that a continuance of racial discrimination would create a racist Frankenstein down the road.

While the Urban League's activities were obviously more favorable to the CIO than to the AFL, the League renewed its efforts to work with the latter. League officials assured the AFL that open support of the CIO was contrary to League policy. Green asked NUL officials to send a memorandum outlining a plan to promote closer relations between the AFL and the Negro community by eliminating discrimination within AFL unions; the League's industrial secretary sent plans for the establishment of a committee on minority group problems to work on racial and religious problems, but this proposal was rejected by Green as "impractical and inadvisable."

The relationship between the CIO and the Negro community proved mutually beneficial. The NAACP actively campaigned for CIO unions and Walter White, NAACP executive secretary, personally aided the United Automobile Worker's drive to organize the Ford Motor Company. White's activities on behalf of the UAW probably helped avert a potential race riot by persuading the large number of Negroes in the plant not to act as strikebreakers in the strike to organize that company. During this strike, the Detroit branch of the NAACP Youth Councils distributed leaflets and White appealed, from a sound truck, to Negroes who refused to leave the River Rouge plant. As a result, enough Negroes supported the UAW or remained neutral to make possible the organization of Ford. For their part, union leaders gave financial support to the NAACP and actively participated in its affairs. John L. Lewis addressed the Association's 1940 convention, and Philip Murray and Walter Reuther became members of the NAACP board of directors. Unions also actively supported civil rights legislation, prompting the NAACP's chief legal adviser to declare that "the program of the CIO has become a Bill of Rights for Negro labor in America." After the Supreme Court desegregation decision of May 1954, the CIO reported that while "the NAACP has taken the leadership in forging the law into an instrument of social precision to accomplish its objectives, the CIO has always been closely associated with the NAACP and other likeminded groups in this struggle." The loyalty of the Negro community was of great advantage to the CIO and the Democratic party in the 1948 national election. Walter White told the 1948 CIO convention, after President Truman had been elected with Negro-leader support, that

> . . . the results would have been impossible for the Negro without labor, or for labor without the Negro vote. It was the job done by organized

labor which narrowed the margin between the two major parties to the point where the Negro vote could be decisive.

White pointed out that the Democrats had won because of 78 electoral votes in California, Illinois, and Ohio in which the Negro vote had been decisive. In California, Negroes cast 60,000 votes for Truman, who won by 31,196. Illinois' 28 electoral votes went for Truman by a margin of 7,968, and he got 120,000 Negro votes. In Ohio, 75,000 Negroes voted for Truman, giving him that state's 25 electoral votes by a margin of 6,817. The NAACP's support also helped unions prevent the passage of "Right to Work" laws in those industrial states with heavy Negro concentrations.

There can also be little question that the CIO's equalitarian position was a factor in causing the AFL to abandon its discriminatory practices and to try to project a more favorable image. During the southern organizing drives launched in 1946, the Southern Organizing Campaign Policy Board, made up of the main AFL leaders in the South, adopted a "unanimous and emphatic" resolution on the importance of special attention to Negroes. The AFL drive added 17 Negro organizers and then adopted a position calling for "equal employment opportunity for the Negro worker and full participation in American Federation of Labor Unionism."

The AFL's unfavorable racial image was not, however, easily overcome, and several elections were lost in the early days of the campaign because Negroes voted for the CIO. In 1946, one of the most important of these election victories established a CIO "beachhead" in Mississippi, when workers at the Masonite Corporation in Laurel swung from the AFL to the CIO by the margin of the Negro vote. After this defeat, the AFL redoubled its efforts to win Negroes away from the CIO. In its appeal to Negroes, the Federation emphasized that it had many more Negroes in official positions than the CIO; that the latter was a Communist-dominated organization; that the AFL had 650,000 Negro members, 450,000 of whom were in the South (which was 50,000 more than the CIO's total southern membership); and that discrimination had been committed against Negroes by many CIO members. AFL organizers contend that this statement was so effective among Negroes in the South that it was used on the West Coast. As a rule, however, while it is probably true that the AFL had about as many Negro members as the CIO, many of these were in segregated or all-Negro locals, and the Negro community was much more favorably disposed toward the CIO up until the time of the merger.

It would be misleading, however, to give the impression that the CIO automatically followed equalitarian policies and got Negro support while all AFL locals discriminated and were shunned by Negroes. Some CIO locals, even in radically led unions like the Mine, Mill and Smelter Workers and the International Longshoremen and Warehousemen's Union (Butte, Montana, and Portland, Oregon, respectively), excluded Negroes from membership. Moreover, Negroes either segregated themselves, or were segregated by whites, in most of the "integrated" CIO unions in the South; in places like Memphis and Birmingham, where CIO affiliates were relatively strong, racially segregated facilities were maintained in CIO headquarters and segregated CIO political affairs meetings were held. Philip Murray was infuriated shortly before his death in 1952 when he addressed a segregated audience of the Steelworkers near Birmingham. When the crowd spilled out of the union hall into the street, union officials gave policemen orders to maintain segregation in the street!

Perhaps the most serious problems for Negroes in CIO unions were the racially segregated lines of progression maintained in most contracts in the basic industries. These seniority arrangements were not entirely the responsibility of the unions, of course, but few unions did anything actively to improve the job opportunities for their Negro members at the plant level. The United Packinghouse Workers were a conspicuous exception to the usual practice. Nor was this problem restricted to the South, because CIO members struck throughout the United States during World War II when Negroes were hired or upgraded into formerly all white organizations. In some cases, CIO unions even lost bargaining rights to AFL unions at least partly because of racial reasons. For instance, the CIO Steelworkers lost the Ingalls Company in Birmingham in 1941 to the AFL Ironworkers because the CIO union had done nothing for the Negro third of the company's work force. Under the CIO, Negroes were denied promotions and their ability to participate in union affairs was limited, but after the AFL won bargaining rights, it proceeded to reclassify and upgrade Negro-held jobs, won a large increase for colored workers, and placed Negroes on contract and grievance committees. In longshoring and the building trades, where the AFL had many more Negro members than the CIO in the South, the CIO was unable to shake the loyalty of the Negro workers to the AFL, even though Negroes were usually in segregated locals. It should be conceded, however, that Negro loyalty to AFL unions in the South was due in some measure to the protection of vested economic interests of Negro union leaders.

And while it is unquestionably true that the CIO enjoyed a much more favorable reputation in the Negro community than the AFL, there is evidence that this reputation was beginning to fade by the time of the merger in 1955. This fact was most obvious in the activities of the CIO Civil Rights Committee, which was established as the Committee to Abolish

Racial Discrimination in 1942, and which helped the CIO gain a favorable image in the Negro community. (This committee will be referred to as the CRC, even though it had other official names.) The CRC was opposed by many international unions which either gave it only token support or ignored it entirely. Some international leaders considered it to be Communist-inspired, despite the fact that the committee was vigorously anti-Communist and actually functioned in part as an organization to fight Communists in other organizations and in the Negro community. Some CIO leaders also argued that the committee was unnecessary because it would merely serve to "smother" rather than solve problems. In this view, racial problems should have been handled through the regular internal union machinery, which had more power to solve them. Moreover, some CIO leaders feared special civil rights programs would split the labor movement along racial lines.

It was clear from the outset that the CRC was to be primarily a public relations organization with advisory powers on racial matters. Members of the committee like Willard Townsend, president of the virtually all-Negro United Transport Service Employees, wrote articles for influential Negro papers like the *Pittsburgh Courier*. It was also clear that the organization had no power or accepted procedures for handling racial cases, but sought "to move in on a racial situation as it occurred" to prevent unfavorable publicity, especially during organizing campaigns.

The CRC encountered difficulties with the Negro press from the start, but the most serious trouble came after World War II when the committee was criticized for being a purely symbolic organization with no power. In 1949, for instance, a writer for the *Pittsburgh Courier* charged that the committee had done little or nothing to overcome discrimination against Negroes. He wrote that in Pittsburgh and other northern cities, the Negro had not experienced "high labor standards" and had "been systematically denied upgrading because of contract clauses which set up discriminatory job line classifications in various plants." The committee should have been abolished, this writer argued, because it "is serving no useful purpose to CIO union members and hasn't even proved itself to be of nominal nuisance value. It is nice window dressing for the organization . . . but in its present form is doing its union and the liberal forces of this country a distinct disservice." This writer suggested that a new committee of elected members be established so that it would be free from the pressures of various union leaders. "Such a program would do much to end the spectacle made by certain CIO officials of color who now hold their offices on a 'puppet' basis."

The *Courier* writer continued his attacks on the Civil Rights Committee and its Negro members in later editions. Concerning the performance of two of the committee's Negro members, includings it director, at the 1949 UAW convention, he declared that "about the only thing missing from the show was a pair of handkerchiefs wrapped around each of the gentlemen's expansive brows."

The *CIO News* and the committee's members issued public statements attacking the *Courier* writer and calling him a "Black Pegler" because he had tried to "smear CIO leaders." But the Negro writer answered that the *CIO News* was smearing "a consistently friendly writer, simply because he found it good and appropriate to criticize certain individuals or practices in the CIO with which honest differences arose from time to time."

These attacks on the Civil Rights Committee caused its members to discuss their public image at the September 1949 meeting, at which Willard Townsend concluded that the committee was "recognized not as a committee to do something, but more like a symbol." Townsend was disturbed because of the CIO's declining reputation among Negroes; he was especially concerned that Negroes in the South were supporting the Communist-dominated Mine, Mill and Smelter Workers, in preference to the CIO Steelworkers. Another Negro member of the committee reported that the "Negro community is saying the Committee to Abolish Discrimination is yes men for the CIO," and they "jump us for being Uncle Toms for the CIO." The CRC's members also agreed that the committee's main problem was its lack of power. The CIO found that its international unions could sometimes be about as autonomous as those in the AFL and that it was difficult for a civil rights committee to halt discrimination in a local or international union without the support of the latter. The committee's only power over local organizations and internationals was moral suasion and expulsion. Moral suasion could be supplemented by publicizing discriminatory practices, but the civil rights committee rejected this because, as its chairman James B. Carey of the Electrical Workers argued, publicity "would injure all unions." Some of the committee members recommended revoking charters of discriminating unions, but the majority of the committee refused to adopt this position on the grounds that it would not solve the problem.

Thus, while there was growing disenchantment with the CIO in the Negro community by the time of the AFL-CIO merger in 1955, we must conclude that the upsurge in unionism in the 1930's and during World War II greatly increased the number of Negro union members. By the time of the merger, moreover, the main Negro organizations in the United States were still basically prounion, Negro-labor political alliances showed little signs of splitting, and Negroes had more strength within the unions than ever before. While precise Negro union membership figures are not available, there were probably at least 1.5 million Negro unionists at the time of the merger. Between 1926 and 1928, there were an estimated 61,000 Negroes in the AFL. Another estimate put 45,000 Negroes in the AFL in 1930 and another 11,000 in independent unions. There were an estimated 600,000 Negro union members in 1940, and 1,250,000 at the peak of employment during World War II. At the time of the merger, Negro union membership probably represented a larger proportion of potential membership than was true of whites, but Negroes were concentrated in a relatively few unions.

AFL-CIO MERGER

It should not be inferred from the previous discussion that the CIO did not, in fact, attempt to pursue equalitarian racial practices. Indeed, we have suggested that the CIO was forced to adopt such policies if it hoped to organize the basic industries where large numbers of Negroes were concentrated. The CIO's policies were also influenced by those of the UMW, which had learned long before 1935 that the increasingly important southern coal mines could not be organized on other than an equalitarian basis. There were other factors influencing the CIO's policies. The CIO was younger and, everything else being equal, the trend in race relations in the United States would lead us to expect that younger organizations would have more equalitarian policies. The CIO had broader social objectives and depended more on third parties for support. The Communists were then making special overtures to Negroes in order to gain Negro support and to use the race issue for Communist purposes, so competition within the CIO between Communists and non-Communists caused the latter to adopt more outspoken equalitarian positions in order to gain the allegiance of Negro workers.[2]

A number of features of the AFL-CIO merger tended to widen the growing gulf between the labor movement and the Negro community. In the first place, two-thirds of the official positions of the merged organization, including the presidency, went to the AFL, which was never able to overcome its unfavorable image in the Negro community and which never had close relations with organizations like the NAACP and the NUL. Secondly, the AFL-CIO Executive Council admitted two unions—the Brotherhood of Locomotive Firemen and the Brotherhood of Railway Trainmen—to the merged federation even though they had race bars in

[2] It is significant that almost every organization that adopted special equalitarian racial machinery either was Communist-dominated or had a strong Communist faction contending for leadership, though this does not mean that these organizations necessarily had *better* racial practices than those—like the UMW—which refused to adopt special machinery.

their constitutions, and none of the former CIO leaders cast a dissenting vote against these organizations. Indeed, only A. Philip Randolph, president of the virtually all Negro Brotherhood of Sleeping Car Porters, an AFL organization, objected to the admission of these organizations on racial grounds. Negro leaders could hardly believe that such CIO civil rights stalwarts as James Carey and Walter Reuther had voted for the admission of organizations with constitutional prohibitions to nonwhite membership. Thirdly, there have been a number of widely publicized legal cases of discrimination against various local unions in northern cities with large Negro concentrations. The Negro community has been particularly incensed at the vigorous defense of discrimination by these unions before fair employment practices commissions, in the courts, and before such organizations as the AFL-CIO Civil Rights Committee and the federal contract committees.

In one of the most widely publicized cases during the 1950–1960 period, for example, International Brotherhood of Electrical Workers' Local 38 in Cleveland refused to accept Negro members in spite of vigorous efforts by the local fair employment practices committee and the mayor. The local finally agreed to admit three Negro electricians in June 1958, after ten years of intensive efforts by the Negro community. The local capitulated only after George Meany told it to admit the Negroes or be expelled, but the union demonstrated its continued defiance by refusing to admit the Negro who brought the charges that finally resulted in breaking the local's racial barriers. Similar action was brought against IBEW locals in other cities, particularly Detroit (where the Cleveland experience apparently softened the local's resistance), Hartford (where the local capitulated, after having defied the state fair employment practices commission, under threat of heavy fines for contempt of court) and Washington, D. C. Washington IBEW Local 26 refused to accept Negro members in spite of efforts by various civil rights organizations, the President's Committee on Government Contracts, and George Meany, who threatened to import nonunion Negro electricians to break the local's racial bar.

. . . While the AFL-CIO adopted a much more liberal racial position than the CIO, the apparent ineffectiveness of the machinery set up by the merged organization led to the conviction that the AFL-CIO Civil Rights Committee, like its CIO predecessor, was mainly "window dressing."

The debates at the 1959 AFL-CIO convention raised several important issues which symbolized the nature of the differences between the AFL-CIO and Negro leaders. The first debate involved a resolution by Randolph and other BSCP delegates calling for the expulsion of the BRT and

BLF unless the latter removed their race bars within six months after the convention. George Meany and all but two other white delegates supported a subcommittee report which noted that the BRT and the BLF had "failed to carry out their pledge to the AFL-CIO Executive Council, made by them at the time of their admission to comply with the civil rights policy of the AFL-CIO," but, instead of establishing a time limit, recommended that the Executive Council be authorized to get compliance "at the earliest possible date." Meany argued that a time limitation would strengthen those within the railroad unions who wanted to keep the color bars. White union leaders felt that discrimination could be more easily removed if the railway brotherhoods were in the Federation. They also argued that the officers of the two organizations favored compliance with the AFL-CIO's constitution, and that this made the race question different from communism and corruption because the latter were mainly leadership and not membership problems. The BRT removed its race bar in 1960, but the BLF refused to do so until July 1963.

The race question was raised a second time at the convention when Randolph unsuccessfully opposed the admission to the Federation of the International Longshoremen's Association (ILA) on the ground that the latter discriminated against Negroes in New York. Meany said that Randolph had never brought the charges against the Longshoremen to the attention of the Executive Council, of which he was a member, or to the subcommittee studying the ILA's admission. Meany implied that Randolph was seeking publicity and said he thought it was time Randolph ". . . got on the team, joined the labor movement, and became part and parcel of the AFL-CIO. To come at this late date, where he has this audience . . . to come up with this material, I don't think that's playing the game. . . ."

But the most heated conflict between Meany and Randolph came over the BSCP's resolution which would have required that segregated locals "be liquidated and eliminated" by AFL-CIO affiliates. Delegates from internationals with segregated locals insisted that Negroes preferred this arrangement and that the internationals would not force them to be abolished. The BSCP delegates argued that segregated locals usually deprived Negroes of equal employment opportunities and were no more defensible because their members wanted them than it was to "maintain unions under Communist domination and corrupt influences on the ground the members of said unions desired to keep them." Meany replied heatedly to Randolph: "Is this your idea of a democratic process, that you don't care what the Negro members think? You don't care if they want to maintain the union they have had for so many years? I would like an answer to that." When Randolph answered "yes," Meany responded

RAY MARSHALL ★ 151

angrily: "That's not my policy, I am for the democratic rights of the Negro members. Who in the hell appointed you as guardian of the Negro members in America? You talk about tolerance!"[3]

Meanwhile, a complex of forces was changing race relations generally. The migration of Negroes out of the South increased their political and economic power, but contributed to their frustration. The many Negroes who came up out of the South during and after World War II found some improvement in their political positions, but continued to face discrimination and segregation untempered by even the slightest traces of noblesse oblige. Race riots, low incomes, charges of police brutality, high unemployment, segregated dilapidated housing, job discrimination, *de facto* school segregation, all undoubtedly contributed to the Negro's disillusionment with the North and greatly strengthened the frustration and hate that builds black nationalist movements. While no one can claim to understand the "mood" of the Negro community, this feeling apparently has been accompanied by growing distrust of white liberals, in the labor movement and out. Another important factor influencing Negro-labor relations has been the growing political power of Negroes as they migrate out of the South and as their power to embarrass the United States in international politics has grown with improved world communications and the conflict over communism. During the 1930's, Negro leaders found it expedient to do business with unions. Now they have less need for the unions and can rely more on their own organizations and the government.

NEGRO LABOR ORGANIZATIONS

Within the labor movement, the status of Negro labor unionists declines as the Negro community becomes disenchanted with unions. In order to counter this reputation, Negro unionists have become more militant and outspoken in their attacks on white union leaders. As a Philadelphia Negro union leader put it:

> We've got to stop Uncle Tomming it. The spotlight is on racial integration and we've got to move while we have the opportunity. If we have to hurt our friends, then we will just have to hurt them. I consider myself to be one of the new breed of Negroes. I'm not begging at the back door for scraps, but knocking on the front door for my rights.

The Negro unionists' growing dissatisfaction with civil rights progress within the labor movement and in the larger community found formal

[3] This version of Meany's reply is taken from the writer's personal notes. The official version printed in the *Proceedings* is substantially the same, but reads: "Who appointed you as guardian. . . ."

expression in the organization of the Negro-American Labor Council in 1960. Organizations of Negro unionists are by no means recent developments, however, because Negro workers have formed caucuses and other organizations to promote their objectives in the labor movement since the Civil War. The immediate prototype of the NALC was the Trade Union Leadership Conference formed by a group of Detroit unionists in 1957. Among other objectives, the TULC sought to become an internal pressure group to direct the power of the labor movement into broad civil rights activities and ". . . to interpret the Negro community to the labor movement and the labor movement to the Negro community."

In 1962, the TULC was instrumental in accomplishing one of its basic objectives by getting a Negro elected to the UAW Executive Board for the first time. Negroes had agitated for this objective within the UAW for over twenty years. The TULC has also brought pressure to bear on Negro unionists who refused to support it by labeling them "Uncle Toms" or "handkerchief heads," and has attacked high-ranking white union leaders. Following the conflict between A. Philip Randolph and George Meany at the 1959 AFL-CIO convention, for example, the TULC wrote Meany:

> . . . to clear you up on the matter that seemed to be vexing you. . . . The mistake you made is that Brother Randolph was not appointed to this high position. Brother Randolph was accorded this position by the acclamation of the Negro people in recognition of his having devoted almost half a century of his life "in freedom's cause."

By the time the NALC was formed, groups like the TULC had been organized in Youngstown, St. Louis, Pittsburgh, Philadelphia, Buffalo, Milwaukee, Cleveland, Chicago, Gary, and New York. . . .

THE NAACP

The changes in the Negro community have also brought growing pressures on organizations like the NAACP to attack the labor movement. The association's victories in the school desegregation cases greatly increased its prestige in the Negro community, but the changes taking place in race relations made it difficult for the association to continue to work closely with organizations (like the AFL-CIO) considered to be discriminatory by increasing numbers of Negroes. In order to maintain its status in the Negro community, the NAACP has had to shake off its image as a "black bourgeois" organization. The association's position of leadership has also made it possible for it to rely increasingly on Negroes and less on unions for financial support. Hence the NAACP has been able to attack AFL-CIO unions for continued discrimination.

The NAACP has recently joined with other civil rights groups to supplement its traditional legal and publicity tactics with pickets, demonstrations, and direct action against unions in order to get more jobs for Negroes. Such action was taken in New York in June 1963, where pickets disrupted work on a $23.5 million Harlem hospital project and got an agreement from Mayor Wagner to help get more Negroes employed in the building trades. The mayor appointed an "action panel" to study the situation and reported that the president of the Building and Construction Trades Council had assured him that Negroes would be put to work "right away" if qualified. The demonstrators and the BCTC refused to accept the recommendations of the mayor's panel.

In Philadelphia, NAACP and Congress of Racial Equality demonstrations resulted in injuries to a number of persons, halted work on a $18 million building project, and got agreements from contractors working on public projects to hire qualified Negro craftsmen. In Philadelphia, Negroes who were employed on the picketed project in certain occupations were pressured by the pickets not to return to work; those who did were photographed and, according to the president of the Philadelphia branch of the NAACP, "will be ostracized by the Negro community." In July 1963 pickets protesting alleged building trades discrimination clashed with police in Newark. The mayor was critical of the organization conducting the pickets, but halted work on the project pending investigation by the Newark Human Relations Council. . . .

IMPACT OF THE NEGRO-LABOR CONFLICT

Against this background, we may appraise the likely future impact of the Negro-labor conflict. Nothing in this area is necessarily predetermined, of course, because the parties involved have the ability to change the course of events.

What will happen to the Negro-labor split? I would guess that it will continue, that discriminating unions will be subjected to increasing regulation by the federal government and the courts, that unions will change their practices when their sources of power are threatened by these regulations, by demonstrations and other pressures from the Negro community, and by alienation of public opinion. Possible threats could be: loss of control over apprenticeship training; decertification of discriminating unions by the NLRB; loss of control over state and municipal licensing provisions where these are used for racial discrimination; loss of control over hiring and referral systems; and being barred from federal, state, and municipal work.

While national unions and federations will respond to these threats, the real problem of discrimination is at the local level. Locals, too, will abolish discrimination if sufficient pressure is brought on them, but this will be a much more enduring problem than getting national union leaders to accept nondiscrimination policies. Moreover, conflict will probably continue because Negroes will charge discrimination where it does not exist or is difficult to prove and because some civil rights organizations will not be satisfied with full equality of opportunity now, even if they get it. They will ask for quota systems and other special treatment which unions are likely to resist.

Trends in all of these directions are clearly perceptible at the present time. For example, most of the industrial states and municipalities where Negroes are concentrated are under constant pressure to bar discriminatory unions from contract work. Moreover, the Committee on Equal Employment created by President Kennedy has moved more directly against unions than President Eisenhower's Committee on Government Contracts. Finally, the NLRB is showing belated signs of taking more direct action against discriminatory unions.

The federal courts have long ruled that unions could not refuse to represent Negroes fairly, even though it was not required by law to admit them to membership. The courts also have ruled that unions are liable for damages and that discriminatory union actions can be enjoined. While the NLRB has consistently refused to revoke certification of discriminating unions, despite repeated threats to the contrary, there is some indication that the Board is responding to President Kennedy's increased interest in equal rights for Negroes by moving in the direction of de-certification of discriminating unions.

A trial examiner in a recent case, for instance, recommended that the certification of an independent union in Houston be revoked because "where a union segregates members or excludes or denies full-membership status to applicants, on racial grounds, it is violating its duty of fair representation to all members of the unit and should not be permitted to hold a certified status." While this conclusion goes beyond the reasoning of the courts, it is based on the cogent reasoning of a minority of legal opinion, that unions which deny membership to Negroes cannot adequately represent them. The NLRB has been more timid than the federal courts in the past, but if it upholds the trial examiner in this case, it will be taking even stronger measures against unions than the courts have been willing to adopt.

While it is too early to evaluate the results, we have also noted the trend by the NAACP and other civil rights organizations to supplement their traditional legal and publicity tactics with direct action, as at Philadelphia, New York, and Newark.

But while there has been some estrangement of Negroes from the labor movement, there appears to be little likelihood that many Negro union members will leave their unions or try to form all-Negro organizations for bargaining purposes. Negro union membership is concentrated in unions controlled by whites, and there is little chance that Negro organizations could operate effectively on purely racial bases. Negro unionists understand the AFL-CIO's power limitations better than the Negro community. They also realize that Negro workers have gained considerable job protection from unions and that they have legal rights to jobs with unions that they would not have on an unorganized basis. For instance, in states without FEP laws, Negroes have no legal rights to equal job opportunities, but where a union is certified, it has a statutory obligation to work to get equal opportunities for Negroes and it has been held that the employer is jointly liable with the union for this duty. In short, Negro unionists appear to believe that the best chance for solution to their problems is not to secede, but to exert maximum pressures within the mainstream of the labor movement.

This is not to argue, however, that the unions' unfavorable image in the Negro community has not hurt organizing among unorganized Negroes. There is growing though inconclusive evidence that Negroes who could formerly be counted upon to support national unions in organizing campaigns are now voting against those unions. Unions have lost some important elections in the South since 1958 because of their failure to get Negro support.

Finally, while the Negro-labor political alliance has also been subjected to the strains in the conflict between the NAACP and the AFL-CIO, there is little indication that Negro voters have turned away from labor candidates and issues, except for some splits in the South. Some of these coalitions in the South had been fairly effective, as in Tennessee and parts of Texas, especially when the race issue was secondary to joint economic interests. In the deep South, however, union leaders were afraid to form alliances with Negroes fearing they would lead to anti-labor laws.

Segregationists have been actively trying to break Negro-labor coalitions or to prevent them from forming for fear that increasing Negro voter registrations and union membership would shift the political balance away from segregationists. Segregationists also realize the danger of these coalitions if legislatures are reapportioned in favor of urban areas, where Negroes and unions could be strong. Negro-labor coalitions are also potentially very important because the growth of the Republican party in the South will divide whites along economic lines and in many areas could give Negro-labor coalitions the balance of power. To counter these coalitions, segregationists have vigorously opposed equalitarian racial policies within unions. They have also sought to split these alliances by supporting prounion segregationists candidates where unions are strong.

In Arkansas, for example, Governor Orval Faubus was elected in 1956 with Negro-labor support. After the 1957 school disorders, unions continued to support Faubus, but Negroes obviously could not do so. Segregationists have not always succeeded in breaking these alliances, however, as demonstrated by the failure in 1960 to defeat Senator Estes Kefauver in Tennessee. On the whole, moreover, while they will not always establish formal alliances, there seems little evidence that Negroes or unions will switch to the Republicans in the South or in the nation. Negroes and unions realize that both would be weakened if the Negro vote returned to the Republican camp and unions refused to back civil rights legislation. This explains why unions have furnished decisive support for the various state FEP laws and why Negro organizations like the NAACP have vigorously opposed the growing support for "Right to Work" laws in the Negro community.

SUMMARY AND CONCLUSIONS

We have seen that Negro-labor relations were strained before the 1930's because of racial discrimination by unions, antiunion attitudes of important Negro leaders, and the strikebreaking roles played by many Negroes. The Negro community became much more favorably disposed toward the CIO, however, because of its equalitarian racial position and because it appeared to be an important emerging power center. For its part, the CIO needed Negro support to organize the basic industries in which Negroes were concentrated and to carry out mutual objectives, so the CIO-Negro alliance proved mutually beneficial. While the CIO did much to improve the Negro's position with unions—and was undoubtedly a factor causing AFL unions to adopt more equalitarian positions—there was considerable discrimination by CIO rank-and-file members and even by local officers, especially in the South. The CIO's failure to eliminate these practices created a growing suspicion in the Negro community that that organization's equalitarian policies were partly "window dressing."

This Negro-labor split widened with the AFL-CIO merger for a number of reasons. AFL leaders (who were even more suspiciously regarded by many Negro leaders than the CIO) gained control of the new Federation. There were, moreover, many widely publicized legal proceedings charging discrimination on the part of AFL-CIO affiliates. Also, the Negroes' increased political power made them less dependent on unions. The NAACP took a more vigorous position against discrimination by unions because of its growing prestige and because of competition from more militant Negro leaders. Negroes also generally are becoming disillusioned because of continuing discrimination against them in the North as well as in the South and dissatisfaction with the rate of improvement in, or actual deterioration of, their economic status relative to whites. Unions are considered to be at least partly responsible for Negroes' economic disadvantages.

. . . While the Negro-labor conflict will probably continue, and might hurt union organizing among Negroes, Negro unionists are not likely to withdraw from the labor movement. Negro-labor political cooperation seems to have been disrupted in some places in the South, but on the whole does not seem to have been disturbed very much by Negro attacks on unions. We conclude that the pressures on unions have caused them to seek to overcome discrimination in their ranks. This can be expected to continue in the future.

SELECTIVE
BIBLIOGRAPHY

Among the survey histories of American labor, the liveliest and the best introduction remains Foster R. Dulles, *Labor in America* (third revised edition, 1966). More detailed are Joseph G. Rayback, *A History of American Labor* (1959) and Philip Taft, *Organized Labor in American History* (1964). The briefest modern survey is Henry Pelling, *American Labor* (1960), which places inordinate emphasis on the influence of immigration. There are two detailed multivolume histories: the pioneering John R. Commons et al., *History of Labour in the United States* (1918–1935), which covers the period up to 1932; and, from a radical perspective, Philip S. Foner, *History of the Labor Movement in the United States* (1947-   ), which carries the story through the IWW and which is still continuing. Among the collections of labor documents, two useful and accessible paperbacks are Leon Litwack, *The American Labor Movement* (1962) and Jerold S. Auerbach, *American Labor: The Twentieth Century* (1969). Maurice F. Neufeld, *A Representative Bibliography of American Labor History* (1964) is the best bibliographical guide for students. Also useful is Fred Duane Rose, *American Labor in Journals of History: A Bibliography* (1962).

For the pre-Civil War period, the literature, although uneven, is quite extensive. Much of it is confined to articles in scholarly journals, the best guides to which are Neufeld's and Rose's bibliographies, cited above. In addition to the first volume of Commons' *History,* which in many ways remains the best narrative for this period, see Norman Ware, *The Industrial Worker, 1840–1860* (1924), William A. Sullivan; *The Industrial Worker in Pennsylvania, 1800–1840* (1955); Walter E. Hugins, *Jacksonian Democracy and the Working Class* (1960); and Philip Taft, "On the Origins of Business Unionism," *Industrial and Labor Relations Review*, XVIII (October, 1963), pp. 20–38. David Montgomery, *Beyond Equality: Labor and the Radical Republicans 1862–1872* (1967) supersedes all the other literature for that period. The career of the dominant figure during that era may be traced in Jonathan P. Grossman, *William Sylvis, Pioneer of American Labor* (1945). The standard account of the conflict between labor reform and trade unionism is Gerald N. Grob, *Workers and Utopia: A Study of Ideological Conflict in the American Labor Movement, 1865–1900* (1961). There is no satisfactory modern history of the Knights of Labor, but students can follow the story in Commons' *History;* Norman Ware, *The Labor Movement in the United States, 1860–1895* (1929); Henry J. Browne, *The Catholic Church and the Knights of Labor* (1949); and the autobiography of Terence V. Powderly, *The Path I Trod* (1940). Philip Taft, *The A.F. of L. in the Time of Gompers* (1957) and *The A.F. of L. from the Death of Gompers to the Merger* (1959) form the standard history of the American Federation of Labor. The older Lewis L. Lorwin, *The American Federation of Labor: History, Policies, and Prospects* (1933) remains a valuable institutional history. Samuel Gompers tells his own story in *Seventy Years of Life and Labor* (1925), which can be supplemented for details and critical comment by Bernard Mandel, *Samuel Gompers* (1963). Lloyd Ulman, *The Rise of the National Trade Union* (1955) provides a brilliant and complex analysis of the development of the national union, the dominant institution on the labor movement. Among the many studies of individual unions, the student should consult Robert Christie, *Empire in Wood* (1956), which best reveals the way business unionism worked out in practice; Mark Perlman, *The Machinists* (1961), which emphasizes structure and government; Seymour M. Lipset et al., *Union Democracy: The Internal Politics of the International Typographical Union* (1956), which looks at internal union politics; and David Brody, *The Butcher Workmen: A Study of Unionization* (1964), which focuses on the unionizing process.

The political stance of the labor movement, with a strong emphasis on the influence of the Catholic Church, is analyzed in Mark Karson, *American Labor Unions and Politics, 1900–1918* (1958). Marguerite Green, *The National Civic Federation and the American Labor Movement, 1900–1925* (1956) describes the abortive attempt to bring about an alliance between labor and big business. The best book on labor in the 1920s is Irving

Bernstein, *The Lean Years: A History of the American Worker, 1920–1933* (1960). The sequel, *Turbulent Years: A History of the American Worker, 1933–1941* (1970), carries the story through the depression in rich narrative detail. Other informative accounts of aspects of the great labor upheaval of the 1930s are: James O. Morris, *Conflict Within the AFL: A Study of Craft Versus Industrial Unionism, 1900–1938* (1958); Irving Bernstein, *New Deal Collective Bargaining Policy* (1950); Sidney Fine, *The Automobile Under the Blue Eagle* (1963); Milton Derber and Edwin Young, eds., *Labor and the New Deal* (1957); Walter Galenson, *The CIO Challenge to the AFL* (1960); Saul Alinsky, *John L. Lewis* (1949); David Brody, "The Emergence of Mass-Production Unionism," in John Braeman et al., *Change and Continuity in Twentieth Century America* (1964); Jerold S. Auerbach, *Labor and Liberty: The LaFollette Committee and the New Deal* (1966). The war decade is treated adequately in Joel Seidman, *American Labor from Defense to Reconversion* (1953). The story of the merger is told in detail in Arthur J. Goldberg, *AFL-CIO: Labor United* (1956). The recent history of the labor movement has not yet been written, but students may begin with Paul Jacobs, *The State of the Unions* (1963); Sidney Lens, *The Crisis of American Labor* (1959); Paul Jacobs and Michael Harrington, eds., *Labor in a Free Society* (1959); Jack Stieber, ed., *U.S. Industrial Relations: The Next Twenty Years* (1959); and, in a study exceptional for its shrewdness and data, Ralph and Estelle James, *Hoffa and the Teamsters* (1965).

Among the books that discuss the treatment of blacks in the labor movement, the student should consult Sterling D. Spero and Abram L. Harris, *The Black Worker* (1931); Horace R. Clayton and George S. Mitchell, *Black Workers and the New Unions* (1939); Herbert R. Northrup, *Organized Labor and the Negro* (1944); and Ray Marshall, *The Negro and Organized Labor* (1965). The role of the immigrant can be traced in Charlotte Erickson, *American Industry and the European Immigrant, 1860–1885* (1957); Clifton K. Yearley, *Britons in American Labor: A History of the Influence of the United Kingdom Immigrants on American Labor, 1820–1914* (1957); David Brody, *Steelworkers in America: the Nonunion Era* (1960); and Gerd Korman, *Industrialization, Immigrants and Americanizers: The View from Milwaukee, 1866–1921* (1967). There is an extensive literature on the radical strain in American labor. On the IWW, Melvyn Dubofsky, *We Shall Be All* (1969) supersedes all previous work. Paul F. Brissenden, *The I.W.W., A Study of American Syndicalism* (1920) remains valuable as an institutional history. David J. Saposs, *Left-Wing Unionism* (1926) contains some still interesting insights. On the socialists, see David A. Shannon, *The Socialist Party of America* (1955) for the background; Daniel Bell, "The Background and Development of Marxian Socialism in the United States," in Daniel D. Egbert and Stow Persons, eds., *Socialism and American Life,* Vol. I (1952); Ray Ginger, *The Bending Cross: A Biography of Eugene V. Debs* (1949); and Henry F. Bedford, *Socialism and the Workers in Massachusetts, 1886–1912* (1966). The study of Communist activity should commence with Irving Howe and Lewis Coser, *The American Communist Party: A Critical History* (1957). Theodore Draper, *The Roots of American Communism* (1957) and *American Communism and Soviet Russia* (1960) are unrivaled for the period they cover. For the later years, see Max Kampelman, *The Communist Party vs. the CIO* (1957) and David J. Saposs, *Communism in American Unions* (1959).